CRISIS

IN THE

ENTERPRISE

Dave Govan

CRISIS

Research shows that over 50% of sales professionals fail to achieve their goals year in and year out. This problem exists in both good and bad economic times and is not getting better. Due to our critical reliance on sales, negative sales performance can severely impact the overall performance results of any private or public company.

ROOT CAUSES

In Crisis In The Enterprise, Dave Govan examines the root causes of the crisis and guides sales professionals, sales leaders, and CEOs to assess the following areas in their own environment:
• Sales Culture
• Core Selling Skills Proficiency
• Training
• Sales Coaching
• Sales Planning
• Human Capital

RESOLUTION

Individuals and companies can significantly improve their sales performance by taking the same approach Govan used to resolve the crisis in his own organizations.

Within Crisis In The Enterprise, Govan shares the innovative management science techniques he created as a leader to overcome critical issues in sales organizations in large, medium, and small companies.

Govan also shares the sales strategies and tactics he used to achieve Oracle Corporation's Global Account Manager of the Year Award as well as numerous other top 10% performance rankings and MVP awards throughout his career.

Ordering Information
Paperback Version available through Create Space/Amazon.com

Production Management: DeMaria Studio
Interior design and page layout: Rusel DeMaria
ISBN-978-1-442-19645-2

Printed in the United States of America

G2 Strategic Advisory Services
improving sales & marketing in the technology industry

Phone: 1.800.974.2230
Web Site: www.g2sas.com

<u>AUTHOR'S BIO</u>

Dave Govan has over twenty years experience in the information technology industry and is widely recognized as a subject matter expert on enterprise sales. Dave is founder and principal at G2 Strategic Advisory Services, a management consulting firm assisting technology industry boards of directors, CEOs, and CSOs on go-to-market strategies and optimizing sales execution. Dave is a former senior vice president of North America sales for VeriSign's (VRSN) Security Services division and senior vice president of worldwide sales for Juice Software (ProClarity/Microsoft). Dave also led sales organizations at Net Perceptions (NETP) and Oracle Corporation (ORCL) and sold for Oracle and Digital (DEC) achieving numerous honors and awards during his distinguished career. Dave is a resident of NJ and is married with four sons.

VISIT US AT

www.g2sas.com

Email: inquiries@g2strategicadvisoryservices.com

Phone:1-800.974.2230

Blog: www.salesadvice.blogsome.com

Twitter: G2salesadvice

DEDICATION

"An honest answer is the sign of true friendship"
Proverbs 24:26

I dedicate this book to all of my friends and colleagues in the technology industry whom I've had the pleasure of knowing and working with throughout my career.

And to all others who invest their time creating, marketing, selling, or supporting information technology products and services for the benefit of others.

CONTENTS

Part IV: Opportunity Management

Part V: Human Capital

Part VI: Crisis Resolution

PREFACE

As I write this, I am seeing an unraveling of our financial industry, as more and more issues come to light about the role our financial institutions are playing in our current economic troubles. But that's not what this book is about. And yet, in a way, it is, because I have a revelation of my own to share.

My revelation concerns a crisis in the information technology industry—an industry of great significance, now and in the future. The crisis that I'm referring to will expand unless something is done. It's not getting better, and I am worried. In fact I'm very worried. Why? For one thing, I'm worried about the impact this crisis is having on one of the most important organizations within a company, the sales organization. And I'm even more concerned about the apparent lack of awareness that a crisis even exists. Because I've spent much of my career in enterprise technology sales, I decided to write this book and try to help. This book is both a diagnosis and a prescription. My goal is to promote a return to the true art and science of enterprise sales, and to encourage the recovery of the values and expertise that seem to have been lost along the way.

During the past two decades, I've had the privilege of working with thousands of sales professionals and sales leaders in the information technology industry. As a member of this community, I have developed a deep respect for its members, and have learned so much from so many of them.

I have shared firsthand the challenges and the rewards of the profession. Like hundreds of thousands of my colleagues in the industry I spent years going to work every morning under the pressure of having to achieve a sales quota. I bet my livelihood on the reliability of products I played no role in developing. I bet my personal reputation and the financial well–being of my family on the strategies of my employers. I carried the responsibility of externally representing my employer in a competitive global market place and interacting with customers face to face. Like my colleagues, I continued to perform my job responsibilities through good days and bad days—days spent in maternity wards and in funeral homes, and everything in between. I learned that a sales professional can't close his or her "door." Even if they are having a bad day, they must be "on," regardless of circumstances in their personal lives.

Like my colleagues I have also dealt with the impact of economic forces beyond my control that further challenged me. I am fortunate that I had the training and adaptability to have achieved success over the years in good and poor economic times. I attribute my success to a strong education in management science and marketing, extensive training, and effective coaching. I am writing this book to share the knowledge and experience I have collected with the hope that it will help leaders and individual contributors improve results.

Over the years though I have noticed changes that I believe have contributed to serious business issues. During the second half of my career, while leading sales organizations, I encountered serious deficiencies in the training of sales professionals. I also observed a deficiency in performance coaching, and I personally experienced how these deficiencies negatively affect sales performance. The purpose of this book is to stop this crisis from spreading further and help improve sales performance across the board.

At executive levels within companies I have also observed a lack of understanding of many important aspects of a sales organization and the issues affecting performance. As a sales leader, I invested the time, money and resources to address these issues within my organizations. However, I want to do more to help the members of the community that I deeply care for and respect. As a leader, I want to do more to increase the overall awareness of enterprise sales organizations and the issues they face. And as an investor, I want to help companies improve the performance of their sales organizations. It is my hope that by writing this book I can make a difference by encouraging companies to invest more in training. It is my hope that companies will adopt some of the management science techniques I recommend in this book to enable more effective planning and coaching, which I believe will improve sales performance significantly. And, although I clearly identify a crisis within enterprise sales, this book is not meant to be an indictment in any way. As I said before, it is a diagnosis and a prescription for better health.

In the following chapters, I provide an insider's candid view of the issues that many sales organizations are facing today, as well as recommendations for how to resolve the issues and improve sales performance. The resolutions are not academic in nature; they are tried and true practical steps that I have used in the real world to help me produce strong results.

As part of the prescription this book offers, I introduce my strategic program for performance coaching called Success Planning. Success Planning directly addresses many of the performance issues affecting sales today, and using it can deliver dramatically improved sales results.

This book also contains stories about actual events I experienced, which I provide to further illustrate the subject matter for the reader. Although I have withheld the names of the individuals and their companies out of respect for their privacy, these stories are true, and they provide good illustrative examples of the issues we face in enterprise sales. Research efforts for this book span my career of twenty –four years, combined with industry intelligence that I have collected during the writing of this book.

I am very thankful to the many friends who have supported me throughout this endeavor. In particular I would like to thank my friend Cris Dolan for encouraging me to write this book. I would also like to thank my lovely wife, Laura, who gave me her support and was very patient while I worked on this project. Lastly, I would like to thank Rusel DeMaria, a very accomplished author, who when I was struggling to find a copy editor and book designer, rescued me by providing those services and went way beyond the call of duty by improving the book in so many ways. I don't feel I could have accomplished everything without his involvement.

The writing and publishing of this book has been a two year journey. I am very pleased to complete this work and share my insider's view with you in the hope that it can affect a positive change in the performance of enterprise sales in the information technology industry.

Dave Govan, G2 Strategic Advisory Services
Bedminster, New Jersey, March 26, 2009
davegovan@davegovan.com
www.g2sas.com

CRISIS

IN THE

ENTERPRISE

Introduction

CRISIS IN THE ENTERPRISE

Would you invest in a company if its sales functions were in crisis?

If the quarterly earnings statement of a company you had invested in stated that more than fifty percent of its employees were consistently falling below their quarterly or annual goals, would you remain comfortable with your investment? Would you continue to invest?

If you're like me, you would be very concerned. And here's the well–kept secret: Enterprise sales is in a state of crisis. This crisis has been building since long before the current recessionary period, and it will remain even when the economy recovers. It will not change until we do something about it.

I've spent most of my professional life in enterprise sales, and frankly, I am very concerned by what I see today, and I want to do something about it. I want to shine a light on this issue and offer suggestions for resolving the crisis. For it is a crisis, and after reading this book you will be wondering how much more revenue and profit companies could be generating if sales productivity were to live to its highest standards and meet its real potential.

To begin with, let's be clear on what I mean by enterprise sales, which I define as selling something that is a reasonably high–ticket item sold to a large customer base. Industry examples are medical instruments, computer software, computer hardware, and so forth. It is in the profession of enterprise sales that I have spent the past 22 years of my life—practicing both the art and the science of sales professionalism and sales leadership.

If you don't believe that Sales is a profession you should probably stop reading now. If you don't believe that Sales is both an art and a science... well, we can get to that in time.

Why would someone not view Sales as a profession? Perhaps it's because not all people who sell have professional standards or skills. Moreover, some products or services simply require a sales contact to take an order or answer a simple question. However you slice it, in the world of enterprise sales you need professionals, and the crisis I'm referring to is a professional crisis.

THE CRISIS DEFINED

Okay. What is this crisis all about? Why do I think enterprise sales is in a crisis?

I have facts and figures, but let's start out with what I have seen firsthand. Having led several enterprise sales organizations in both large public and small private companies, I have seen changes–changes for the worse–in the sales arms of many companies. I also carried a bag for twelve years, so I have experience from the bottom to the top of the sales force chain. And it's not just me. I've spoken with many business executives, and there is nearly unanimous concern and complaining about sales–related issues, such as slow sales growth, poor pipeline management, lack of forecast visibility, lack of forecast accuracy, lack of cross–selling, small deal sizes, sales attrition, high loss ratios, low morale.... I could go on, but let's just say that there is a general feeling that the quality of the performance of sales professionals has dropped dramatically in the past ten years when compared with the previous twenty.

It's not about the economy, for once. Our current economic downturn is the third I have seen in my career, and they don't correlate with the problems of enterprise sales. Take a look at the following research studies, which indicate that the issues plaguing enterprise sales have been building for some time now and are not isolated to the current recession.

In 2004, the CSO Insights' Annual Sales Survey* questioned 1,337 companies worldwide and found that 51% of sales reps failed to make their quota last year, marking the first time in the report's 10–year history that a majority had missed its target. Seven in 10 companies said that their "close rate," the ability to land deals after making sales presentations, was less than 50 percent.

In 2007, the TAS Group's TAS Index Global Sales Effectiveness Benchmark Study† found that more than half of the companies surveyed report fewer than 50% of their sales people making quotas.

Surveys are useful, but it's also easy to see the problem simply by reading the news reports. In the news, it becomes clear that sales performance issues are bedeviling companies throughout the technology industry. Here's an earnings disappointment from January of 2008 citing poor sales execution:

CEO says Quantum Itself is to Blame for the Vendor's Q3 Disappointment‡

By James Rogers,

Despite growing talk of recession and an IT spending slowdown, the exec refused to blame macroeconomic conditions for Quantum's performance. "We felt that it was pretty focused on our execution, and pretty central to North America. We haven't seen business dry up or see deals come off the table... There are many actions underway to address this revenue challenge," the CEO said, highlighting Quantum's decision to focus attention on its sales teams and pre–sales engineers.

---

* http://www.csoinsights.com/current_reports.htm
† http://www.thetasgroup.com/tas/resources_tasindex.html
‡ http://www.byteandswitch.com/document.asp?doc_id=138983

Here's an example from July 2007:

Compuware dumps president after Q1 profit warning

By Tony Baer

Citing extremely poor sales execution, Compuware issued a profit warning for Q1 and got rid of its president and COO as a result.

Chairman and CEO Peter Karmanos placed the blame on extremely poor sales execution. In a Q&A with investment analysts, Karmanos said that the extent of the drop didn't become apparent until the last few days of the quarter, when expected sales never materialized. "It absolutely blew us away on how bad the quarter ended up."

Here's an example of an earnings release blaming poor sales execution:

SEATTLE—November 2, 2007—Insightful Corporation (NASDAQ: IFUL), a leading provider of predictive analytics and reporting solutions, today announced its operating results for the third quarter ended September 30, 2007. Insightful reported total revenues of $4.9 million in the third quarter of 2007, a decline of 16% when compared to revenues of $5.9 million in the third quarter of 2006

"We are disappointed with our results for the quarter," said Jeff Coombs, president and CEO of Insightful. "We continue to feel that our strategic direction, to deliver packaged predictive analytic solutions built on an enterprise–scale S–PLUS platform, remains sound. However, we suffered from poor sales execution. Our lower revenues for the third quarter were in part a result of turnover in critical sales functions, of focusing too early on long sales cycles for products and solutions that have not yet been released, and of not closing the larger deals in our pipeline. We also saw declines in our professional services revenues, as custom projects dropped off in anticipation of product releases of packaged solutions."

What about large technology vendors? Let's look at an example from an Earnings Call by Oracle Corporation, in December of 2006:

> Oracle Corporation (ORCL)
>
> F2Q07 Earnings Call
>
> December 18, 2006 5:00 pm ET
>
> ....As we have looked at the new license results, we believe it basically came down to execution on a number of deals that did not close in the quarter. These were not competitive losses either in technology or in apps, and these deals should close in Q3...
>
> We think that additional focus and better pipeline management should result in higher conversion rates and much better execution in the third quarter. Focus to us means reducing the time spent on internal meetings and non–core sales activities, leaving the field more time to work with customers and close deals."

Can you see what happened here? While Oracle is known for having one of the best sales organizations in the world, even they are suffering from problems of sales execution and a lack of effective pipeline management. Putting it more plainly, you might say that some sales professionals failed to exhibit the highest caliber of professional work. Further, despite how the release is worded, I would guess that the slippage from the forecasted quarter was most likely not an execution issue but a qualification issue. The reality is that unless there is a sudden and extreme change of events, the actual closing and booking of a sale should be a simple and straightforward event, as I will explain in a future chapter.

In a case like the one described above, I would question whether the business was far enough along to forecast for the quarter. The customers were probably not ready to buy and the usual end–of–quarter discount incentives did not matter. So, given the situation, what's a sales professional to do? The answer is, there is plenty to do. Although I will offer more detail later, for now, let's look at some simple concepts.

First, don't forecast business that isn't going to close. Qualify the heck out of the sale to make sure you are solving *pain* that is "acute" enough. There is value in solving the pain, but the person you are solving the pain for has the ultimate decision–making power. Is your customer's plan to buy your product now or in three or six months? In other words, are they acting on active pain, which is strong enough to motivate them to take action and buy something now, rather than passive pain, which allows them to delay the purchase decision? For those not part of the sales professions, this is what we call the Sales 101 level of qualification in enterprise sales.

What about Sales Management? Don't they have a responsibility here also? Of course they do. They probably acted as if a high percentage of their "Pipeline" consisted of quality data. They probably used a statistical forecasting approach based on hunches or historical trends that predicted x percent of their pipeline was going to close in the quarter. If they did that, they probably screwed up! In the chapter on forecasting, we will discuss how they can improve their methods and their accuracy.

Apparently, there are problems in the sales sector, but not even those who are reporting them seem to recognize the root causes of the crisis. IN this book, I invite you to look at some of the specific issues that have contributed to the current situation.

Part I

Culture, Values and Professionalism

By now you understand that I am trying to call your attention to real problems in today's enterprise sales profession. There are numbers to indicate that the problem exists, but what's behind those numbers? Let's look at several of the elements that contribute to the performance issues within enterprise sales.

Chapter 1

SALES CULTURE

I'm sure you are aware that all companies have an established culture unique to their work environment. If the culture is aligned with adding shareholder / investor value that culture can be an asset. Additionally, subcultures may exist within a company culture. In the case of the sales function, sales professionals thrive when the subculture they are working in provides a sufficient level of support, compensation, and recognition. I'm not sure why, but sales professionals are extremely sensitive to the sales subculture of the company they join, and after they join, whether or not the culture is changing for the better or the worse. Perhaps they invest in the culture because they are buying into a dream or a vision when they are hired. They are very understandably sensitive whether their dream can become reality or is merely a pipe dream.

Of course, like anyone who buys into something, they go through a period of cognitive dissonance. When joining a company's sales organization, in reality they have bought into a laundry list of elements that define that company: a long term strategy and a strategy toward competition, a short term business plan, a managerial style, commission opportunities and rules, the quality of the products, employee stock projections, financial viability and so forth. In reality, all employees who join a company are buying into the same things, but sales professionals are uniquely betting on these basics plus their own personal brand, past customer relationships and forty to sixty percent of their compensation, to name a few specifics.

Sales leaders who hire sales professionals are not just staffing open headcount they are selling *Dreams* with a capital D. They are selling the potential of future success and future higher W2s to their candidates. In

11

addition to the financial aspects of their compensation plan, enterprise sales professionals are looking to join a "sales culture".

A sales subculture is made up of many elements of the company's sales philosophy and methods. Here are some of the elements I've seen in positive and productive sales cultures:

- Pay for Performance
- Compensation Plans with Strong Upside
- Making the numbers are expected "table stakes"
- Frequent Recognition of Wins
- Accepting of Results Not Excuses
- Customer Satisfaction Driven
- Teamwork Oriented
- Competitive
- Work Hard / Play Hard

In contrast here is a list of elements that characterize a non–sales culture—one that is not conducive to the work of successful sales professionals:

- Sales compensation plans with little leverage on over achievement
- Internally focused. Many reports.
- Many internal meetings on strategy but weak tactical execution
- Bureaucratic
- Leaders rarely engaged with Customers
- Very Political
- Low on Accountability
- Low frequency of recognition
- Continual missed numbers and low results

Of course sales cultures can also contain negative and counterproductive elements, such as :

- Arrogance
- Overly aggressive with customers, particularly during closing

- Internal battles and destructive rivalries over customers and opportunities
- Disrespectful attitudes
- Too focused on the short term
- Primarily a tactical approach

A company's sales culture is inspired by its leaders; they set the tone and create the working conditions. Hiring good leaders who can instill the positive elements of a sales culture can have dramatic results that lead to success. As you can imagine, hiring the wrong leaders can have the opposite effect. The good news is good leaders can act as cultural change agents, so even when there are existing problems, they can help turn things around.

Leaders should always examine the culture of their sales organization and make sure that it is aligned with the company's strategy. In addition, the company leaders should stay well connected with their top sales performers. They should be aware of any changes occurring within the sales culture—for better or worse—which could be affecting their performance. They should be ready to encourage the positive changes and help ensure that the positive elements of the sales culture flourish. By doing so, they will very likely see lower than average attrition rates.

Some changes are natural, and sales professionals will roll with them, except those that have a negative effect their sales culture. A lack of recognition, unsupportive sales managers, missed numbers, weakened sales compensation plans, lack of focus on customers... any of these changes will erode the confidence of your enterprise sales professionals and may result in the loss of your best sales professionals. Moreover, when your top people leave, it can have a trickledown effect, leading to further attrition. The best enterprise sales talent often follows strong sales leaders who are individual contributors and strong sales managers. If those individuals move on then others will follow.

Don't forget the positive effect of recognition. One very easy way to encourage a more sales–oriented culture is to ensure that your people are recognized in numerous s ways—informally via email and formally every quarter and at the end of the year. What should you recognize? Difficult competitive successes, new customers signed, performance against numbers... These are all good reasons to recognize sales teams. I refer to sales teams because success comes from teamwork. All of the functions that contributed to winning and keeping a customer should be recognized, i.e. sales, presales, order management, legal, finance, support, consulting, alliances, etc.

While on the surface culture might seem like some intangible quality, it is important to respect the impact, both positive and negative, that your culture can have on the performance of your sales organization. This impact can swing quickly in one direction or another, based on your choice of sales leaders.

What makes a good sales leader? One quality that good leaders have is their values.

Chapter 2

VALUES

Everyone has values—tenets and beliefs about how life should be. In the sales profession, values are what I would call a "first quality" issue. If you ask the effective leaders of just about any organization about the importance of values, you will get similar answers: Values are critical. Values are the foundation. Values are everything.

In the sales profession, why are values so important? To begin with, sales professionals must first sell themselves, then sell their company, and last sell their product. In each of these three aspects of sales, values are implicit. Each sales professional must have personal values. Each company has its values, and even products represent values, both to the company and to the customer.

The good news is the majority of sales professionals with whom I have had the pleasure of working have exhibited strong personal values. On the other hand, I've also come across too many people in sales who did not represent and practice the established values of their company. In such cases, it was often that their self–interest overrode the well–being of the customer and the company, and so these individuals only succeeded in representing one of the three values necessary to be a great sales professional.

What's the root cause of issues related to core values?

Clearly, there's no single explanation for the diversity of human behavior that presents itself in how sales professionals approach their jobs. It seems obvious that influences such as family dynamics, school experiences, previous employment, religious beliefs and other factors are relevant. People's personal ethics vary, and often simple greed self absorption or a few dozen other personality traits can affect how people approach their work.

In my opinion, however, while there may be many root causes, there is only one cause for the failure of values to be clearly integrated in the workplace, and it points directly toward leadership. The company leadership is responsible for communicating the company's core values *before employees are hired*. They are also responsible for a management style that supports and reinforces adherence to those values. That's where the buck stops.

Even where management is clear about company values, there will be challenges, and yet, to establish the most professional sales force, it's necessary that leaders meet those challenges. Let me offer an example.

I previously worked at a Fortune 1000 corporation that had established a great set of values and lived them. We all lived by these values, myself and each of the vice presidents who worked for me. However, we often dealt with issues with some of the sales executives who did not adhere to all of our most important company values.

For example one of our most important values was integrity. One particular sales executive seemed to interpret his values differently, and often would get completely hammered at internal or customer events and proceed to piss people off. Telling my boss, "Go F@#$ yourself" was this guy's idea of humor. Obviously not the best display of character or integrity.

The problems with this guy finally reached a climax at an exclusive resort where I was hosting a VIP Customer Loyalty event. As was often the case, he began drinking upon arrival and proceeded to drink himself into oblivion. He had to be physically carried back to his room by two of his customers. How's that for Customer Service? Not what we had in mind, I can assure you.

Now, if the situation were reversed, and he had helped a customer back to his room, that would be, in our view, adding value—doing a service. I've been in that very position, and my assistance was always appreciated. However, what's at issue here is that company events, whether private or public, are *work*. Our sales executive seemed not to recognize that he was a host, and instead made himself into a dysfunctional burden, an embarrassment to the company and, no doubt, to his customers.

I was not present to witness these goings–on. I was in another part of the resort enjoying some relaxation with some other customers. I learned about the incident the next day, and, as the company's leader, it was my responsibility to take action and to uphold our company values. On Monday, I publicly informed my organization that we recently had an "incident," but I did not mention anyone's name. I did, however, use the incident as a reminder to our employees that we each have a responsibility toward the company—that each of us is expected to act consistently with our company's values and to represent proper business decorum. I also reminded them that it's not about us, it's all about the customer.

Later, I spoke with the responsible (or should I say, irresponsible) individual one–on–one. I listened to his side of the story, which consisted of an embarrassed apology. I was compassionate, knowing that he was terribly regretful and suggested that if he had a problem he should seek help. I also informed him that there will be zero tolerance for such behavior going forward and that another such incident would result in his termination.

The conversation was effective in that he clearly understood the consequences he faced, and he was able to clean up his act. However, the story doesn't end in storybook fashion, because he really didn't represent the values of the organization. In truth, I didn't see him having a long–term future with us, and when, a few months later, he came and demanded a promotion, he resigned when his demand was not met.

In the end, this man's values were an obstacle to achieving success and did not meet the values of the company, and he found his own way out. However, as much as I am a fan of customer entertainment, one lesson from this incident is that it is "playing while working," not an out of control frat party.

Getting back to the subject of values, I have my favorites. These are some of the values that I think should most matter to people in the sales profession:

Empathy: Putting yourself in another person's shoes—in this case, the customer. What is important to them? What are they risking? What do they gain? What does each buyer really care about? How do they like to communicate? How do they like to be sold? Understand your customers and what they want and need. Listen to them; they will let you know if you are listening well enough. A sale is really not about talking; it's about responding after listening. It's about asking open, probing questions, which give you an opportunity to listen. So, in the case of sales, listening is the key to empathy.

Truthfulness: Don't lie to customers. Don't try to sell something that doesn't exist. Any time you lie, they will figure it out eventually, and your commission will get clawed back. The irony is that customers sometimes lie to their sales contacts. There is even an old saying that "buyers are liars". Customers will often make up a story to mask why they bought from someone else or why they did not buy from anyone yet, or about their personal buying power or authority. However, this isn't about customers' values, it's about yours. Your value is to be truthful, whatever the customer may do or say.

For instance, don't lie about your pipeline or your forecast. If you are struggling, be an adult and admit it. Where there's a problem, take a problem–solving approach with your manager. Try to figure out what is impeding your success. And if the problem has to do with your work ethic, lying will only postpone the inevitable result–reduced income or termination.

(Lying on your resume is not a good idea either. On several occasions I have experienced outright falsehoods created by sales candidates, but we'll look at employment issues later, in Chapter 20: Staffing.)

Passion. If you don't believe passionately in what you are selling, you should look for another job immediately. It is paramount that you believe in what you are doing and what you are selling. If you don't have passion for your work and your product, the people you approach will pick up on it. Without passion, you will never succeed. Also, life's too short to spend your time doing something that doesn't totally pump you up.

Quality of Work. Strive for excellence. Make sure everything you do reflects high quality. Your performance is a reflection of your personal brand. Remember, you possess nothing more important in the workplace than your reputation. I got this message early in life. My grandmother used to tell me that your "good name" is priceless, and can never be taken from you unless you allow it to be. Words to live by...

Accountability. Follow through. Do what you say you are going to do. Don't tell someone you will get back to them tomorrow if you are going to be out of the office. Set realistic expectations that you can meet or exceed. This is important internally, as when you are forecasting, just as it is critical to your customer follow–up.

Sense of Urgency. If you don't have a sense of urgency, you need to develop one. You are working in a very competitive global marketplace, and customers prefer to deal with as few sales executives as possible. They will love to give you their business if you're the one who is fulfilling their requests for information, pricing, and so forth quickly and accurately. Be the one with the fastest turnaround of high quality information and recommendations. That's how you get, and keep, their business and their loyalty. They will know you are working harder–for them.

Integrity. I already mentioned integrity and offered one example, but there's more than one way to demonstrate integrity, and that is in how you view your customers. If you have the customer's best interest at heart, they will trust you much more than other vendors. If you don't try to sell them things they don't need or oversell them or nickel–and–dime them they will learn to trust you. That trust will often lead to a closer relationship, in which they share more information with you. They may even offer you some tips and coaching on how to "win" with them and with others.

All in all, values provide the foundation for the rest of your game. Professionals who exhibit solid values combined with other proficiencies, in most cases, will succeed.

To an extent this may sound like "motherhood" and "apple pie". Of course it does; these are common values we generally share in society. So why are we still repeating the same issues and failing to meet these values consistently? Why doesn't the sales profession jump to the front of the list when the average person thinks of values–based professions? Can we change that perception and ensure that the sales profession becomes known for strong values in the future? Perhaps yes. Perhaps no. It may even be impossible to change public perception. What I do know is that it won't ever happen if we don't look at what we are doing today and become accountable for our actions—for our game—if we don't adhere to a strong values code.

Our personal values are one key. The other is leadership. Leaders need to lead; they need to teach their teams by example and by reinforcing solid values. You may question whether values can be taught, but I believe they can be modeled and taught. As a leader, you can communicate your company values and you can insist that employees live up to the company's standards in their job performance. If you communicate strong values and live up to them yourself, you will thrive. Your employees will know that if they don't follow your lead, they won't survive here.

Talking the talk, walking the walk, and incorporating values as one of the benchmarks of your sales professionalism starts at the top, from the Chairman on down the line to each individual. Without consistency, the credibility of a firm's values decreases. For instance, when all the employees and leaders in a company are taught to adhere to strong values and manage within the law to establish a positive work environment and avoid sexual harassment suits, but the Chairman is a playboy who frequently dips his quill in the company ink, then the value system loses credibility. Lead from the top, by example, and you'll have the moral high ground and the legitimacy to expect the rest of your company to follow suit.

Chapter 3

PROFESSIONALISM

What is professionalism? Does that mean something concrete? Let's look at what we often notice about someone who says, "That's a professional." First, by definition, we see someone who is being paid for his or her talents and expertise, and the higher the pay, the more "professional" we assume that person to be. This may conjure up images for you of people you have known who were the best at what they did, whether it was science, art, trade skills or sales. You have probably met many of these individuals during your lifetime—perhaps even someone in your family. Besides making money, what was it about that special person that made you think of them as "professional"?

Was it:

- the way they greeted you?
- the way they spoke?
- the way they were dressed?
- their manners?
- their air of confidence?
- how they performed their job function?

My guess is it was probably all of the above.

Let's simplify this a little. Looking at the short list above, all of the traits we might have attributed to a "professional" were also traits that we admire or that we like in people we know. So, without getting into sociological debates about the relative merits of certain personality traits, we can probably agree that the professional is someone who makes a good impression on us. We might further agree that we buy things from people we like, and we like people who are pleasant, courteous and well mannered toward us. We like doing business with people who are well dressed and well groomed. We communicate best with people who listen to us and speak clearly with us. We like doing business with competent people who deliver what they commit to delivering.

I may be accused of being "old school" on professionalism, but doesn't this just seem like common sense? And while it may seem obvious, no one is born with "professional" attributes. We learn them. I learned them from my parents, my teachers, and from formal training.

The first comprehensive sales training program I experienced that touched on professionalism was at my second job. One day our instructor came into class and handed us a small booklet on professionalism. I was three years out of college and had been working in a corporation up to this point. My first reaction to the booklet was not favorable. *I am already a professional*, I thought. *What else could I possibly need to know?*

The answer was, plenty. I had the idea, initially, that my company was trying to turn me into Miss Manners, but in actuality, they were working to ensure that I was on par with the best sales professionals in the business, not to mention the executive level customers I would be working with. I didn't know what I didn't know, but they did. They taught me for good reasons, too, because I was working for a large corporation that was in competition with a dozen other large corporations. My company wanted to make sure that their sales representatives could match or exceed the professionalism of their competition, thus eliminating any potential advantages their competitors might enjoy.

Some of the basics of professionalism that are important in sales are as follows:

- **Be on Time.** Don't arrive late; on the other hand, don't arrive too early. Arriving to a meeting 10 minutes early is acceptable, unless you have to clear security at a location separate from your meeting place. Plan ahead. Make sure you have enough time to check in or whatever you might have to do and still be a few minutes early for your meeting. Be sure to reserve time for unexpected traffic delays.

- **Be Friendly.** Be amiable and outgoing, but not pushy. Introduce yourself by shaking hands with the individuals attending the meeting.

- **Business Cards.** Formally present your business card and allow them to present theirs.

- **Come Prepared.** If you are giving a presentation, determine in advance who is providing the projection equipment and who, specifically, is setting it up. Do this preparation work in advance of the meeting. In such cases, make sure you are 30 minutes early, that you have access to the equipment/room, and that you are prepared to test your presentation and equipment. Test your laptop, above all, to be sure you can set it up to project. I can't tell you how many times I've watched nervous people fumble around as a meeting is starting.

- **Grooming.** It's simple. Be well–groomed.

- **Attire.** Be well–dressed. Recommended: Conservative business suit and tie when presenting or meeting with those in power.

- **Sun Glasses.** Despite how cool you look in them, don't wear sun glasses into the building.

- **Personal Hygiene.** Don't do it in public. For instance, don't comb your hair in the lobby. (I've witnessed someone doing just that.)

- **Gifts.** Don't offer holiday gifts unless you are certain the customer's company policies allow them to accept gifts.

On the gift–giving issue, if you think I'm exaggerating, I can put you in touch with a certain sales representative who worked for me several years ago. He did all of the above when hosting me at a meeting with the CIO of a Fortune 500 retail account. I questioned the gift issue in advance, but he ignored my warning point only to end up red–faced embarrassed when the CIO handed back to him the cheap bottle of wine with our company logo on it. It was our first meeting with the CIO, and not only were we embarrassed, but so was he. The moral is: no gifts unless you're sure it is acceptable policy.

- **Demeanor.** Speak clearly, be friendly, and confident.
- **Conversations.** Be a good listener. Do not cut off the other person when they are speaking. Pay attention to the conversation and stay on topic. Listen with all your attention, as if there was going to be a test later, which there may very well be.
- **Local Customs.** If you are visiting another country or people who follow different customs than you are used to, learn those customs and do your best to observe them. For example, Japanese do not like aggressive arm waving or similar movements. They also like business cards presented with both hands on the card and a slight bow making eye contact. Check out *Do's and Taboos around the World*, by Roger E Axtell (of Parker Pen Company), John Wiley & Sons, Inc. It's a great reference book for learning these kinds of customs.
- **Check Your Work.** Spell check all written communication except for instant messaging. Spell check emails, documents, letters, quotes, etc. The work you produce is a reflection of yourself and your company. Typos signify a lack of attention to detail and a lack of quality, and they are easily avoided.
- **Be Composed.** Never lose your cool with a Customer. It's okay to get fired up and passionate during a negotiation, but never express anger.

CORE SELLING SKILLS

Many people think that sales is easy. You just follow up on leads, call people, get them to meet with you, show them what you have, and ask them how much they would like to purchase. Right? Piece of cake.

Does that sound naïve? I have experienced many senior executives in non–sales functions who believe this myth. Even the people who are running sales–oriented businesses often tend to over–simplify the reality of the sales process. Everybody buys things; we are all customers, and for most people that is the perspective they use to understand sales. They assume that the customer at the enterprise level is similar to them, and that sales works the way they have experienced it. In Part II of *Crisis in the Enterprise*, we'll take a closer look at the all-important core sales skills and what is missing today.

Part II

Core Selling Skills and Leadership

Chapter 4

WHAT'S GOING ON IN ENTERPRISE SALES?

Previously, I referred to the sales profession as a combination of art and science. As in any serious profession, there are many job–related proficiencies required in order to be successful in enterprise sales. Still, more proficiencies are needed by the leaders of enterprise sales teams.

At the most basic level is a set of Sales 101 level proficiencies, which are known as the five basic stages of selling—Prospecting, Qualifying, Presenting, Negotiating, and Closing. As basic level proficiencies, these seem straightforward, don't they? Yet I contend that it is deficiencies in these very core selling skills that are contributing to the crisis we face today. Why is that?

It's time for another dirty little secret. As simple as it seems, core selling skills proficiency has dropped dramatically over the past two decades. You can ask just about any sales leader or sales recruiter. I have spoken with many of them, and they agree with me.

It's something I've seen in every sales organization I have ever been a part of. If I were to generalize I would say that most sales professionals are proficient in two of the five skills, and those proficiencies they have mastered varies according to the individual. I'm sure you've heard of the "closer" in your group. Well, in my experience, the closers were not always the best at prospecting or presenting. In contrast, the best presenters are often not the best closers. The point is that individuals gravitate to their natural areas of strength. Perhaps it is human nature to do so, but this kind of specialization is not what sales is all about. Imagine you are an airline pilot and you are only really strong at taking off, but you're not so great at landing. Or you can land all right, but you can't seem to keep from stalling out your plane while flying. Not a very good pilot, and likewise, a sales person who can only close, or who can only present, is missing core skills. He's likely to crash and burn somewhere along the way.

What happened? How did a whole generation of sales professionals end up with serious core deficiencies? There is actually a simple explanation: In the 1960s, 1970s, and 1980s, large corporations—companies like Xerox, DEC, IBM and HP, among others—hired young college graduates into sales and trained the heck out of them.

Starting in the late 1980s and continuing to the present day, important training programs have been significantly cut back. Despite the increases in global competition, we have created a generation of less fully trained, less proficient sales professionals. This is not to say that every sales professional today is lacking skills. Of course not. There are people we know who make their millions in enterprise sales, even today, but in many cases these are people who have natural talent and often they are self–taught. Ever hear of the 20/60/20 rule? I've heard trainers use that term to refer to the idea that 20 percent of the people already get it and just need support, 20 percent at the bottom will never get it and need to change jobs, and the sweet spot for trainers is the 60 % who can be taught to get it, adopt it, and make a difference. I have seen similarities outside of training, though I haven't seen enough investment in helping our knowledge workers in sales.

And I do believe that college–educated sales professionals are *knowledge workers*, by which I mean that a knowledge worker is someone in an organization who takes information and adds value to it—uses it to accomplish an important task or function. For instance, they are the ones who win new customers and provide the life blood, called revenue, to pay for all the other functions of the company.

If you can agree with me that sales professionals are knowledge workers, then how much training have they received in their life, or in a given year? Were their core skills ever tested for retraining?

"Hold on," you might say. "How did they get their job in the first place, if they are lacking core skills?"

Let's take a trip down Memory Lane and recall the *dot com* boom of the late 1990s, which ended in early 2002. It was a "tech gold rush," during which there was an extreme shortage of trained sales professionals, and a rising demand. College graduates would immediately enter the workforce and join a start–up company, receiving higher salaries and compensation plans than ever before in the history of sales. After a year or two of surviving in a company under the most favorable conditions, they could change jobs and demand a $90K base salary plus commission and be making $125K to $200K. Yes, that is correct. Within two years of graduating they could be well into six figures.

Many of these new graduates also were hired for business development functions. Business development is an important function, but it differs from direct sales. The market did not seem to care, however, because many individuals who started in "bus dev" naturally moved over into sales roles. Is there anything wrong with this picture? I would say yes. What was missing is what the earlier generation of sales professionals got in good doses—Training, with a capital "T". Most of these companies provided very little, if any, training.

Over time, many well–trained older sales professionals retired or moved into sales management, though others did continue in their sales roles. However, the next generation of sales professionals are "training orphans". They soon found themselves working for individuals who had received training early in their careers. The new generation did not have the same foundations. Since then, some managers have risen from the new generation, particularly during the dot com boom, and they also lacked the background and training of the experienced professionals.

I've mentioned core selling skills several times, but not taken the time to describe them in any detail. Let's take a deeper look at what it takes to be a successful enterprise sales professional. Understanding what's required will help us see why the current crisis exists.

Chapter 5

SALES PROSPECTING

Sales prospecting is just like any prospecting—you're hoping to unearth some gold or, in the best of cases, discover a motherload, but you won't discover anything if you don't have the knowledge and the tools of your trade. In the case of sales prospecting, you have to engage in cold calling, develop solicitation telephone skills, give mini presentations and become adept at handling objections. It's also important to work with, through or around executive–level assistants and to be able to get through voicemail screens to speak with a live person. These are among the many skills involved in sales prospecting, skills that I believe too many of today's sales professionals lack.

It's not that sales prospecting is being ignored. While I was writing this book, I Googled "sales prospecting" and received 1.2 million hits. The hits were mostly for books or companies with books and systems on how to improve your sales prospecting. I did find one company that was taking a different approach with a system that made the claim, "Never Cold Call Again". I could have spent $97 to learn how that's possible, but I didn't. My assumption, however, is that the author is suggesting an improved approach based on high–quality lead acquisition and or referrals from existing customers. Thus your sales prospecting efforts are not truly "cold" because you are dealing with a "warm" lead. The key issue here is that sales professionals need to do more prospecting and be more profi-cient at prospecting to be successful.

Frankly, all a sales leader really cares about is that you have a pipeline of real opportunities that you are working on, aka your *sales funnel*. Your sales funnel should equal approximately two to three times your quota. We will go into the metrics later, but for now, let's say we don't care how you do it. My issue is that most sales executives don't meet these standards, and if they aren't doing it, what *are* they doing? I guess they should prospect more.

It's common to blame marketing for not producing enough leads or giving sales bad leads , but at the end of the day the marketing team is not as highly leveraged in their compensation as you are. They are probably paid a decent salary and a bonus based on the corporate bonus pool. If more of their compensation was tied to objectives (MBOs) per se, such as lead generation, pipeline size and actual sales it would be a different story. I won't hold my breath for that to happen anytime soon, however, so at the end of the day, as we say on the street, "They don't hold your wallet, you do".

If your pipeline is insufficient, it's up to you to take action to increase it. Marketing *may* be able to assist you, but not necessarily. Once again, at the end of the day, your spouse won't be disappointed with the marketing guy if you bring home less money. Any disappointment will be directed at you. Trust me.

The good news is that sales prospecting is a learnable skill. One great reference is the work of Paul Goldner, *Red–Hot Cold Call Selling: Prospecting Techniques That Pay Off*. (AMACOM, 1995). There are dozens of other books on effective cold calling and sales prospecting, so I'll leave it to you to explore them, should you want to delve deeper into the subject.

The problem today is that, whether it's a "cold" lead or a "red hot" lead, there's still a serious deficiency in our profession, and yet it's a weakness that mostly goes undetected. Unless you are in an inside sales job your core sales prospecting skills will most likely never be screened, evaluated, or reviewed. A common, but false, general assumption is that if you have been in enterprise sales, then you must be great at prospecting.

Sales candidates, when asked in interviews how proficient they are in this area, naturally tend to answer in the positive. Some hiring managers will ask for a mini presentation as an example of prospecting, but very few will ever drill down and ask the candidate to phone them and treat them like a "suspect". (A "suspect" is someone you contact to qualify further and turn into a "prospect" — someone you qualify deeper and try to engage in your selling process.)

I will admit that, as a sales leader, I have only put a few candidates to this test. I also will admit that I had a soft spot in my heart when they were doing it, and I find myself wondering why I didn't do a better job of screening. Perhaps it has something to do with the very healthy egos common to most sales professionals, which on the positive side allows them to deal with rejection and the ups and downs of their trade, but on the flip side can make them more touchy and easily insulted. Imagine asking a star professional football player to show you how they put on their shoulder pads and the rest of their gear during an interview for a spot on the team. It is just assumed that they know how to do such things. It's inconceivable that they would not know how to put on their own equipment at that level, and it's equally inconceivable (on the surface) that a sales applicant would not know the basics of sales. And yet they often don't have the skills of their trade, and their deficiencies are not revealed in interviews that fail to test their abilities.

There's no real excuse for the lack of sales prospecting skills today, especially when you take into account all the books and resources available to sales professionals on the Internet, such as the prospecting tool, "Jigsaw" (*www.jigsaw.com*) or a networking tool like LinkedIn (*www.linkedin.com*). The trick is to encourage and train our sales professionals without insulting them. Training experts no doubt have their own ideas, but common sense tells me that if training (or re–training) is approached as a "tune–up" course that's required of everyone in sales within a company—sort of like the continuing education required of medical and psychological professionals—it could work.

Another, even better approach may be to make it very specific to your company and their products. Make it a mandatory for every new hire. To make it stick, require sales leaders to reinforce the training in each of their groups, or individually with their people. The bottom line? We can't continue to ignore the issue. The cost of customer acquisition is too high. Sales productivity needs to improve and it all starts with sales prospecting.

Who is potentially your greatest ally when you are working your leads and your prospects? If you answered executive administration assistants, you get a gold star. If you work for a Fortune 1000 company, chances are you will know the name of the CEO's assistant long before you will know the name of many of the functional leaders, and you know better than to upset them. What about your prospects and customers? Do you know *their* executive assistants? Do *they* know you? What do they think of you? If they don't know you, you have a problem, and you need to fix it. If this is a new account, then you need to make this relationship a priority.

As a sales leader, when I'm asked to assist on an opportunity or account, I will inevitably ask an account executive if they know the executive prospect's assistant. The best sales executives always do. The worst never do. Some people think, *I want to deal with as few individuals as necessary since time is money so why bother? She or he has no power.* Hah! If you really believe that you have no idea where the power lies.

Everyone in business is really in the people business, whatever they are making, selling or providing. Executives are leaders of people, so who helps the executive communicate with his/her people? Who manages their incoming and outgoing communications? Ah yes. The assistant. And time is money, so who schedules the executive's time? Again, the assistant. And when approvals are required there is often a lot of paperwork and internal communication, so who handles that? You know the answer, and I think you get the point. Next to the executive prospect or customer, there is no more important person to you than his/her assistant.

So how do you relate to the assistants? It's certainly *not* by treating them like second class citizens. To begin with, at an executive level, they are often smarter than we are, and if they are treated well by the executives in their own company, which is usually the case, they aren't likely to take kindly to being talked down to, bullied or disrespected. Personally, I have always had tremendous respect for the job they do and have treated them accordingly. When I carried a bag and handled large accounts, I made sure we knew each other by name and face. I made sure they knew I was a good business partner who would never cause conflict or screw anything up for them or their boss. I also made sure I showed my appreciation for our relationship with a card or flowers, or something special during the holidays. To be clear, I wasn't trying to date them. I was just showing respect for a very important member of the virtual team of customers and my team. Sometimes they treated ME like a second class citizen, but I sucked it up and treated the relationship like gold. Once I proved myself in their environment they usually softened up.

You may be saying to yourself that this is interesting, but it is not something one can teach, that it's something that has to be learned on the job—in the field. In part this is true. In part it comes from having genuine respect for other people. But it works. I have even gone so far as to ask my own assistants to speak to my sales executives and offer tips or advice on how best to relate to people with their responsibilities and position on the customer's side. The experience was uniquely and bilaterally rewarding. My assistants appreciated being valued and enjoyed helping the team out. The team was reminded of an important relationship and asset. Why not schedule a training conference call and engage some of the executive assistants in your own company? They deal with outside vendors fairly often. They know what works and what doesn't. They often prioritize who gets time with their boss, and when.

Chapter 6

QUALIFICATION

There are numerous definitions of sales *qualification*, the second of the five basic core proficiencies. Simply defined, it is a process by which interested parties, AKA "suspects," are determined to be qualified prospects. Prospects are the ones we should devote time to, to turn them into customers. The essence of effective qualification is to determine if your product or service adds value to the prospect's business, fits within their environment, and aligns with their plan from a budget and timing perspective. There are multiple levels of qualification, such as technical fit, customer fit, and so on. Let's take a closer look.

As a starting point, the folks at Value Vision netted it out nicely in their *eValuePrompter* approach: Qualify for Pain, Fit, Value, Power, and Plan.

Let's put this in the form of questions:

- Does what you're selling address relevant "pain" in the suspect's business? Simple examples: cut costs, increase productivity, reduce time to market...

- Does your product fit the need?

- Does it fit in the technical environment?

- Does the value you provide justify the cost of your product and its implementation and maintenance?

- Are you dealing with the appropriate people in the hierarchy? Can they make the decision to buy?

- When do they plan to buy and how much? When do they want to start the project?

* www.evalueprompter.com

39

Meanwhile, the folks at *www.salesexcellence.com* back in 2001 reminded us that qualification should not stop at the beginning of the sales cycle. "It [qualification] is an integral part of the ongoing process itself. So, as conditions change throughout a sales campaign, an opportunity could easily be qualified one day, and not qualified the next. The purpose of sales qualification is to determine the "quality" or close–ability of each sales opportunity in our pipeline in order to prioritize our efforts and properly allocate sales resources."

At this point, I would agree with you if you are thinking that sales qualification seems straightforward. If so, where's the crisis? Do we still have a problem?

Again, the issue is not so much in a complete lack of ability, but in the degree of proficiency currently being demonstrated throughout the enterprise sales profession. I'm referring to the fact that most sales executives know *how* to qualify, but they are not necessarily good in practice. It's a distinction between knowledge and application. Qualification is a skill that has to be practiced at the highest level of proficiency. Getting a 95 on a exam in school is a solid grade, but qualifying something only 95 percent may result in the loss of a sale or, at best, slipping a deal to the next quarter and delaying your income. This also can have a direct and severe impact on forecasting, as I will discuss later.

Some people mistakenly feel that any sales activity is good activity, and as a consequence, there is also a medical condition that has made its way into our profession. It's called "Happy Ears". People with "Happy Ears" may be asking the right qualification questions, but often only hear the happy answers. The sales executives suffering from this condition are so full of optimism and excitement that they don't pick up on the "flags" the customer is communicating. Or, to stay happy if they do encounter a danger signal, they avoid drilling down into the "danger" zone—the topics that they really should be exploring and examining because they can cost them the sale.

In many cases, the problems have to do with timing, so the sales executive hears that a sale is probable, and overlooks issues of timing. What I know is that adding new opportunities to the sales pipeline *this quarter* makes everyone happy—myself, my spouse, my manager, his/her boss. "Hey Dave, great job on your pipeline size!" "Thanks. I've been working really hard and it's gotten pretty big." Not, "Dave, how come you missed that sale? Weren't you listening to the customer?"

I'm going to go out on a limb here and observe that pipeline size and eventual sales bookings are the equivalent of "penis envy" in the enterprise sales profession, as in, "Mine is bigger than yours." As a sales leader I wish we could replace that attitude with forecast accuracy. After all, isn't it better to qualify out of opportunities that don't fit upfront than to spend time on something that will never close? You probably think I am full of it for flagging this as a problem, but I am telling you, it is a big problem.

Here's what I mean: Even sales executives who know how to qualify and who are often successful throw "pipe dreams" into the pipeline. I like to refer to these ideas as "visions," because these are often the 10% qualified items at the beginning of the year, like new products forecasted in existing accounts. There's nothing wrong with having such visions. Let's just treat them realistically. Treat them as a creative knowledge worker's hope of selling something new to an existing customer. On the other hand, let's not call them qualified opportunities.

I suggested earlier that forecasting accuracy is possibly more significant than pipeline size and sales bookings. Why? And why do you think most sales opportunities slip from one forecast to the next? It's simple. They were never accurately qualified. It was not ascertained whether they would close in the current quarter or at a later date—if at all. We'll see, when we talk about forecasting, that this is significant.

Returning to the issue of qualification, what I've discovered is that the easiest qualifiers are *pain*, *fit* and *value*. The most challenging qualifiers are *power* and *plan*. But even when evaluating pain, fit and value, there can be issues. For instance, is the pain sufficiently acute to motivate a customer to buy something?

I once had a sales executive try like crazy to sell a new service. He spent an entire quarter doing everything he could to sell it. He ran an effective sales campaign. He got to the right people, He ran proof of concept pilots. He created a compelling buy–now offer. He worked hard for those sales, yet he failed to close a single one. When I asked him why, his assessment was that the pain the service addressed was not acute enough. *Wow*, I thought. *What a great way to view the issue.*

It wasn't that the product didn't solve pain, it was that the customer's pain was not acute enough. The customer's pain was passive, not active. In terms of real pain, it was more of an occasional muscle ache than a severe and nagging toothache. I took this information to the EVP of worldwide sales and enlisted his support in removing that product and quota from our channel. In this case, it wasn't just one sales rep who had problems. Several experienced and successful reps had tried—and failed—to sell this product. It was the guy who dedicated his whole quarter to selling it, however, who hit the nail on the head. The pain was there, but it was not acute pain. In layman's terms, the customer's motivation was too weak to yield a sale.

In some companies, product development, engineering, and marketing create "Field of Dreams" products, i.e. if we build it they will come. Unfortunately, this is not how it works in the real world. Real–world customers buy products that solve relevant and active pain, not products that are, for instance, an extension of a service that someone thinks would be cool. So it's not a matter of just determining if a product solves a problem or helps accomplish something. It has to balance out in the value equation. Is it worth the effort to buy and install, etc?

Why are power and plan more challenging qualifiers than pain, fit and value? To start off, let's define what we mean by power. As per my friends at The Complex Sale, Inc. in Atlanta, GA, in a complex sale or an enterprise sale there are almost always a number of individuals, and more importantly, a number of roles involved—specifically, gatekeeper, evaluator, recommender, influencer, approver, decision–maker and signer. In many cases, one person may fill several of these roles, for instance, as approver/decision–maker/signer. However, the higher the value of the sale or project, the higher the likelihood that each role will be represented by a different individual within the hierarchy. To make it a bit more complex, depending on the buying culture of the company, the power could reside near the bottom. A case in point is Lucent, now Alcatel Lucent—formerly Bell Laboratories—where a member of technical staff is empowered to make the selection of a technology and the CIO or CEO cannot overrule it. I believe this to be the exception and not the rule, since most corporations have a top down power flow. Still, in enterprise selling, *all* of the roles are very important and have to be sold to effectively.

I can't tell you how many times I've asked a sales executive if they are working with power on the opportunity, and I have been misled. The answer is always yes. No sales executive wants to admit they could not get to power. Is it really that difficult to figure out who holds the real power? More likely, it's about "being gate kept" or "being blocked".

Sales executives will have a specific point of entry into a company, either proactively generated or as a reaction to being contacted. Customers often assemble project teams and divide up vendors for a primary contact among the project team members. If your contact can be won over, they can become a valuable coach – and "inside" coaches are very helpful. However, sales executives sometimes fall into the trap of what I call "clinging to the coach". This is where they get stuck. They are unable to gain access beyond their point of contact. Part of the problem is that their subsequent communications with their manager tend to be overly generalized and imperfectly relate the level of commitment of the company, precisely because they aren't dealing with the power. They might say, "GE wants to do this," "GE wants that," or "GE needs this," while in reality all of the information they have gathered is from one person's perspective, and that person may be, essentially, a gatekeeper, not a decider. How can one person represent the perspective of all of the divisions of GE anyway? Unless of course that person is at the top of GE's management hierarchy.

I hope I don't insult anyone by saying this, but sometimes "buyers are liars". The sales executive may ask their contact who is involved and who has the decision–making authority. "Who makes the decisions around here?" At least in the early stages, and sometimes for the duration of the sales cycle, you will be told, "Yes, I have power," "Yes, I am important," "Yes, I am the 'Man'". It is this kind of misinformation or misrepresentation that underscores the importance of account intelligence, overall account knowledge and experience when staffing for sales assignments or when selling to enterprise accounts.

Knowing the players and being able to mention other individuals and/or a past experience helps keep everyone honest. There is another effective method at dealing with such situations, which is through Hierarchy, AKA Team Selling, which we will cover later.

Usually, a sales executive finds out that they have not been dealing with power when their "coach" notifies them that another vendor has been selected and "there is nothing I could have done since my manager's manager made the decision, and I really want you, but I'm sorry, I can't afford to commit career suicide." The lesson here is that coaches are really important, but "clinging to the coach" can result is lost sales, missed forecasts, and other bad outcomes.

I like to say the only plan that matters is "Power's Plan". March to that plan and you won't fail. Unless of course power is lying, which is possible. This is why the best sales executives validate what they hear from every level of customer by cross–checking it with other sources of information in the customer's environment. The best source is a customer ally, as well as other customers in that company, other installed–base vendors, and the like.

Assuming you are being told the truth, and you are hearing it from power, then you should know the accurate timing of your opportunity. Why is timing key? Because companies are measured on a quarterly basis and forecasting accurately within a quarter is very important.

Another pitfall we often encounter involves budgets. It's not uncommon for a sales executive to ask if there is a budget for the project, and how much it is. They may find out that there was a budget, but it has been reallocated to another project of higher priority. They'll tell you, "Thank you for asking. At the present time, we have allocated that budget to another project, but we will let you know when your project has been reactivated," or something like that.

What could the sales executive have done to avoid this issue? One strategy is to ask up front what fiscal priority your project has to the customer's department or division, or to the company as a whole. I would ask that same question up and down the management chain. By doing so, you find out not only if there is money, but your overall prognosis for success. If power has not planned to allocate budget to the area you are targeting, then a sale will not occur.

On the other hand, what if the person you have been working with has misrepresented their authority? As I've said before, it happens all the time, and sometimes finding out who truly has responsibility for the decision can take quite a bit of effort. And to be clear, it's not just rookies who sometimes get blindsided by this issue.

This example features a star enterprise sales veteran, someone for whom I have tremendous respect, who committed a one hundred and fifty thousand dollar opportunity in his forecast. His manager, who I respect equally, committed it to me. We all committed it, right up to the CEO in our forecasts. The veteran, was in the final stages of the sale, wrapping it up with the customer's procurement group. We thought that all was well, but all was not well.

Of course, we later identified a serious misstep we had taken – or rather, a serious step we had *not* taken. Earlier in the quarter, during an opportunity review, the veteran's manager and I both reminded him of the importance of an introductory meeting with the CIO, to make sure he qualified the opportunity at the highest level. We had all agreed on this step, but, unfortunately for all of us, this meeting never happened. Based on input from his main contact, the veteran had been lulled into believing that the CIO of this Fortune 1000 corporation would not get involved in a transaction of this size. He wrongly assumed that the meeting would slow down his close. He was already working with procurement. It was a done deal.

Based on what he knew at the time, it sounded like a reasonable assumption; however, it was a false assumption. It turns out that our top competitor had found out about the sale, arranged a meeting with the CIO (the meeting we never had) and convinced her that she should do business with them. Of course, the CIO picked up the phone and directed procurement to stop working with our veteran and instead engage and complete the sales with our competitor. Ouch!!! In our business we like to say that we make "blood" commits, meaning someone will lose a body part if the commit does not come in. In this case the veteran had done an excellent job throughout the sales cycle, but neglected one very important player in the hierarchy, the final approver/real decision maker.

Our conversation afterwards was indicative of the respect he had already earned in his professional work. He spoke of his regret for having blundered, especially knowing how I held him in respect, and expressed his embarrassment. I, on the other hand, reassured him that I still believed in him, but asked what he had taken away from this experience—what he had learned. It was a rhetorical question, but I had to underscore the learning opportunity. If the situation had been different, if this had happened with someone without the veteran's demonstrated high level of competency, I would have taken the person to task. It was a costly mistake, and I would want to be sure that any relatively new sale executive never forgot it.

As a sales leader, I could not help being frustrated after presenting a best–practices approach that was not followed. Of course, this happens in all parts of life, from parenting to coaching athletes, for instance. However, in contrast, I don't think it happens much in engineering. It seems to me that the principles of physical engineering are fully accepted by engineers, who tend to adhere to them strictly, for which I am generally grateful. If engineers were as slipshod in their application of engineering principles as many sales professionals are, we would have reason to be very nervous every time we crossed a bridge. However, we rarely consider that engineers, builders, and inspectors would not follow the best practice approach for bridge design a hundred percent – not 95 percent, which equals bridge collapse and disaster.

It is true that lives are generally not lost when an enterprise sale is lost. On rare occasions, individuals involved may be fired; however, there are costs in the form of lost revenue, lost income, the impact on morale and the opportunity cost for the time spent on a lost sale versus a closed sale. The point is, there are tried and true practices for enterprise sales that can increase your probability of winning. Someone has to lose of course, but I would rather win, and I certainly would not want to lose because of ineffective sales execution.

The point of this whole section on qualification is that there are a lot of ways it can go wrong, and that best practices need to be followed, like the bridge building engineer, one hundred percent of the time. If these practices are followed less than a hundred percent, you can bet that something will happen more than five percent of the time. Remember, qualification is "king". Of all the core sales skills, it has my vote as the most important. Regularly chasing opportunities that are not a fit or have timing issues can kill a company.

The only way to assure that qualification is a fully understood skill is through professional training and retraining. In fact, two levels of training are required: general sales qualification level that is not specific to a product, and product–specific qualification training each and every time a new product is launched.

Leaders of sales and marketing have got to wake up to this issue. I'll say it again: Anything less than one hundred percent proficiency in this core skill is simply *unacceptable*. There are vast external training resources available in the industry to assist if the resources are not available internally. The most common objections to training are time out of the field and money, but to me, it's not even worth debating. Companies cannot afford to have less–than proficient enterprise sales executives. Talk about time and money. A little prevention is worth tons of cure.

Chapter 7

PRESENTATION SKILLS

The third core skill in the sales profession is *presenting*. When most people think about the sales profession, it is presentation skills they are most likely to consider. Sales professionals are expected to have strong communication skills, and if you are in a sales occupation, then you probably have had a training course on how to give an effective presentation. Again, if this is the case, then where is the issue? As with the previous proficiencies, it comes down to the *level of proficiency*, as well as consistency across the profession. In enterprise sales, a sales executive must have at least the flowing four presentation proficiencies:

- **Elevator Pitch**—a thirty second distillation of the business you are in, what you sell, and why an executive should be interested—in other words, the value proposition.

- **Company Overview and Customer Visits to HQ**—the ability to describe your company and their strategy both informally and formally.

- **Product Specific Presentations**—detailed presentations of features, function, and benefits as they relate to the resolution of relevant pain.

- **Proposal Overview Presentations**—informal walk throughs of a proposed solution or service.

This book is full of "dirty little secrets," and here's another. Many sales executives who believe they are good presenters are not strong in *all four* presentation areas. They often hide their weakness by relying on other team members to do their work for them, particularly presales resources. Having had presales as part of my organizations in the past, I consistently heard complaints from presales that sales executives were leaning on presales technical presenters to give the entire sales presentation.

Formal presentations are very interesting to experience, no matter what side of the desk you are on. If you have had a seat at the table or the podium in the past, I'm sure you could tell a few classic stories. Perhaps it's that opening joke that went bad, or maybe it was "experiencing technical difficulty, please stand by". (I wish I had a blood pressure monitor when that happens. Who ever invented those in–focus projectors so that they flake out just when you are ready to start?) Then there's the "angry" pre-senter—the one who got heckled early in the presentation and, for the rest of the presentation seemed to go down "Angry Lane". Or how about the guy in the bowtie we hired to present at our worldwide sales kick–off meeting—the one who gave a great presentation, but insulted half the audience by telling inappropriate cultural jokes?

There are lots of train–wreck stories about presentations gone wrong. One of my favorites is one I heard secondhand from another VP who called me to complain. It seems that one of the reps in my organization fell asleep and was snoring during a presentation to her customers. When asked later what happened, she offered the excuse that she had recently joined the Rescue Squad and was up all night on an emergency. Our later discovery that she tended to consume large quantities of alcohol on a reg-ular basis seemed a more likely explanation, and we addressed her prob-lem by asking her to fall asleep somewhere else.

One of my presales friends used to create product features on the fly during a presentation to overcome objections from prospects. That was an interesting issue to deal with after the customer installed our software.

Train wrecks can be instructive (as well as painfully amusing), but let's talk about how to do presentations right. During interviews, I would often ask the candidate to provide an impromptu company overview and/or a "chalk talk" describing the solution they were selling at the time. I can't tell you how many sales professionals turned pale when asked to provide such a basic demonstration of their presentation skills. I remember when I was asked to provide the final "quality assurance" for sales candidates from a company we had recently purchased. In individual interviews with their top three sales representatives—I asked each of them to go to the white board and do a chalk talk to convince me that I should buy from their company versus our company. Each was visibly nervous and one turned completely pale.

The candidate ranked as the lead candidate blew the presentation. I ranked him last and informed the manager that I would not approve an offer for him. The other two candidates were okay, with one performing a bit better than the other. Since they only had one product to sell, I would have expected a better presentation from each of these "top sales representatives". I'm sure we could offer a few dozen excuses that would explain the root cause of their subpar performances, but, frankly, I am not interested in excuses. The bottom line is most that sales professionals are expected to have strong communication skills, and with basic training, drilling, and review, they can become very proficient.

The other thing I have found to be completely strange is that the best presentation content I've found in the large companies where I've worked was at the CEO level. The CEO's direct reports always had the latest and best content in their slides, and, in many cases, they gave the best presentations. So what's strange about that? The point is, why not also share the best content with sales? Sure, CEOs and their staff present at conferences with hundreds of people in the audience, but day in and day out, the primary external touch point for the company is the enterprise sales force. Why are they not armed with the best content? Why aren't they prepared to give the best presentations?

All right. It wouldn't surprise me if the leaders of many large corporations think, "That's not our problem. We have it covered." Really? Review the competency level of your sales force and chances are you'll see firsthand what I'm talking about. Can they pass the test? In all four areas of competency? And then what?

Let's consider what competency really means. Even if a sales executive is fully competent in all four of the presentation skills I've listed, are they closing the loop? What are they doing to assure that their presentation is going to be successful? How many sales reps interview all or most of the attendees prior to the presentation to determine their specific level of existing knowledge of their company? Their company's technology? Their market and all the other important factors that determine how they will respond to the presentation? How many determine beforehand which specific topics are of interest to the target group?

Suppose there isn't an opportunity to explore these issues before the presentation. Then how many reps ask up front, right at the beginning of the presentation? How many reps allow the prospect/customer to explain their specific goals for the presentation, and actually listen, instead of spewing *speeds and feeds*? I'm afraid I have seen far too few.

The point here is that a sales presentation is not a check box. It is one of the most important facets of the sales cycle, and if planned for and managed appropriately, it can contribute significantly to winning. Even if you are not trying to close a specific opportunity, this is a valid approach. You may simply be hosting an important prospect or client at a visit to your headquarters, but even then, proper planning and preparation are key.

Here's an example: In one of my jobs as a global account manager, I hosted the CIO of a Fortune 25 company, with his staff of eight direct reports at our Customer Visit Center. I treated the event like a formal project and planned accordingly over a period of ninety days. And even though I had two other reps working for me on the HQ location of the account, I took personal responsibility for the agenda, the presenters, the logistics, and even the seating chart. I went so far as to change the layout of the conference room from classroom style to boardroom style. I was making sure the seating was conducive to having a collaborative meeting. Furthermore, I personally made sure the CIO's kosher breakfast and lunch were ordered and attended to properly, and that they were delivered sealed. I made sure my team and I were standing outside the entrance ready to greet our guests when they arrived.

As they arrived, an executive director friend of mine informed me that the previous day's visit to a larger computing vendor had been a travesty. The CIO had wound up lecturing his hosts on what it takes to provide high–caliber enterprise level support. My customer friend warned me that this had better be good! I assured him it would be. The pressure was on, and I was thankful I had taken it so seriously and attended to all the details.

Thanks to the great job of our virtual team of corporate executives, presenters, staff, and my field team, our guests gave us the highest ratings. And, during their visit, they heard enough about our future plans to help pave the way for a very large enterprise sale that would close several months later. They came away feeling great about the relationship between our two companies at all levels. In this case, the company overview was a formal one–day strategic discussion at our headquarters.

I have seen this same level of quality on corporate visits from many of the individuals I have had the pleasure of leading. Unfortunately, I have also seen very poor quality, and my point is there is no excuse for it. Corporate visits are an area where companies need to do more on quality control, as well.

As I mentioned earlier, I'm not trying to compete with formal sales presentation training. On the other hand I am suggesting that we raise the bar with regard to our expectations of sales professionals. At a bare minimum they should:

- Deliver a clear and crisp 30–second overview of who they sell for, what they sell, and how a customer would benefit from their products or services.

- Exhibit quality presentation skills ; demonstrate poise, make eye contact, show patience when asked questions, use good verbal tonation and inflection, be enthusiastic, and so forth.

- Dress in a professional outfit and avoid distractions such as jingling items in their pockets, etc. In fact, learn to use their hands effectively to make their point and reach the audience, not reflexively or nervously.

- Do as much prep work as possible before a formal presentation or demo by interviewing attendees beforehand to determine their interests and issues.

Chapter 8

NEGOTIATION

Whether it is getting to "Yes" or starting with "No," or your own personal positional negotiation technique, a high degree of competency in *negotiation skills* is necessary for all sales professionals. Once again, I have consistently found that these necessary skills are lacking in organizations. You might say about negotiation skills among today's sales professionals *that some are stars and many should be behind bars*—locked up for giving away too much because they did not know how to negotiate. Of course I'm exaggerating for effect, but the reality is that, instead of being *locked up*, these deficient sales reps are *locked out* of the empowerment they require to succeed.

It's not my intention to impart or teach negotiation skills in this book. That is far beyond the scope of what I'm intending, and, in any case there are scores of books and training courses on the topic. I just want to bring attention to the problem of negotiation skills in our enterprise sales forces. Look at it this way: If we didn't have a problem, then why would we require managers to engage so often? Or why would we have the discount approval levels locked down so tightly? Pure and simple, it's because most companies do not and cannot trust their sales executives to negotiate effectively.

As I said before, the best reps are genuinely skilled negotiators. That's part of what makes them the best; however, many sales professionals do not demonstrate the necessary skills. I can't tell you how many times my management team and I have been amazed to hear certain reps insist that we were going to "blow" the sale if we did not give away the store. Because they didn't understand the principles of negotiation, they panicked and wanted to close on unfavorable terms, and in almost every case they were wrong.

I truly do empathize with them, however, because they are taking the heat and their lumps first-hand while many of us are in the "rear with the gear". This is one of the reasons I would always volunteer to help by visiting the customer or getting on the phone with them. If we required approval from a marketing leader or GM of a line of business, I would also encourage that the sales rep host that person live or on the phone with the buyer.

One example of support I provided was when a rep came to me troubled that a VP of marketing she was dealing with just wasn't listening or dealing with reality in a negotiation, and in this case she was right. Our rep had negotiated with Citigroup to double her volume and requested a lower price from our VP of marketing internal approver, who was insisting on a per-unit price increase. The customers were thinking, Let's see, we are buying twice as much and you are RAISING the price? Haven't you people ever heard of *economies of scale*?

My coaching to the rep in this case was to ask that the VP of marketing fly to New York to meet face-to-face with CitiGroup's VP of procurement and explain his flawed logic in person. That tactic worked, because our marketing VP told the rep he was too busy, and he approved the discount. We did not give the store away, but we provided a discount that satisfied both parties in the end.

Enterprise sales requires sales reps who are savvy negotiators. Citigroup has extreme buying power, and they wanted steeper discounts, so the rep led them to significantly increase their quantity. Sounds like a win/win to me. She did not just roll over and give away more, gaining nothing in return.

Despite the problems I perceive today, I don't find negotiation to be an area of vast complexity. It is an area of sales in which a little can go a long way. A little attention and review from management would help drive consistency of quality across our teams, although some training may also be called for. What most concerns me is that the subject of negotiations may be seen as a "sacred cow," meaning that management doesn't want to insult the teams of sales professionals they manage by reviewing or calling into question their negotiation skills.

The fact is, while negotiation is not the deepest of subjects, there is some depth to be plumbed, and sales professionals today are not doing enough to keep their skills honed in this area. How many individuals have gone to the second or third level of training in negotiation? Harvard University has been studying negotiation, for a very long time. The book "Getting to Yes," is a good read about their studies and findings on the subject. I learned quite a bit by reading it and studying different approaches to negotiation. For instance, I learned to recognize when *principle–based negotiation* is superior to *positional negotiation* and have never looked back. With the fierce competition of the global marketplace, we need every edge and advantage. We can't afford to be second, because second in sales doesn't take home any commissions.

Let me give you an example of the competition today's sales reps face:

I recently worked in the information security industry and learned that there were 900 companies in the industry with less than $10 million in sales. This is not a good situation. It is an indicator that the companies are not expanding. There could be a number of reasons, however, we know lack of sales is one of them. I don't know how many sales professionals are deployed across the 900 companies, but I would assume that there are at least several thousand. Imagine that there were really large vendors in the same space. There are also several large vendors competing in the space with significant numbers of sales reps deployed. Add presales technical resources and post–sales consultants, and the number of professionals competing on behalf of their companies just in one sector of the IT industry easily breaks the ten thousand mark. Move over to the software industry and the numbers grow immensely. Getting back to the 20/60/20 rule, if we can have a positive effect on sixty percent of the sales professional in the technology industry, you can imagine the impact.

Further, if our job is to increase value for our shareholders by winning and closing business, then it's probably worth the time to review the skills of our sales forces and strengthen those skills where needed.

Chapter 9

CLOSE PLANNING

Close planning is simply figuring out the who?, what?, when?, and how? of winning a sale and obtaining a signed contract and purchase order. Believe it or not, I've seen time and again how people forget to attend to the details by asking their customers how it works in their company. . This may sound like a minor point, but if close planning is not done effectively, it can kill your quarter. Every sales professional needs to understand how long it is going to take to complete a contract process and who is involved with contract completion and fulfillment within the customer's organization.

CLOSING

"Coffee is for closers," Alec Baldwin proudly announces to Jack Lemmon in the infamous movie *Glenn Gary, Glenn Ross*, which depicts the activities of vacation real estate sales reps. This movie has made such an impact that it was even quoted in another movie, *Boiler Room*, which depicted people in a Wall Street "chop shop," referring to the sales ABC, "always be closing." You may also have heard the famous anonymous quote, "Nothing happens until someone sells something."

Clearly, a lot of emphasis is placed on closing, and not only in the media. If you carry a bag for a living, chances are you are often asked by your peers, "What did you close this quarter?" or, "How much did you book?" If you are a sales professional, these people are not interested in how well you are doing in your personal life. They want to know how much money you are making so they can contrast their own performance with yours. They are taking your measure as a sales professional—comparing their own performance against yours.

Many of us have seen the résumé highlight that says, "Strong Closer" "Many large deals closed," and so forth. And no wonder, because when we think of strong closers in the business world, we think of people like Donald Trump, Ross Perot or Tom Hopkins.

In my experience, almost all sales professionals I've met had some ability to close. I have met a small number who could not, though, to be honest, that's probably because they lacked the basic attributes for being in sales in the first place. For instance, they did not know when to start closing, when to stop, how to close out the conversation, when to stop talking, etc. Of course, I have seen people with superior closing skills, too.

I have my own way of looking at this issue I think that closing is the easiest part of the sale, but why? It's simple, really. If you have executed an effective sales strategy and have done all the necessary upfront work of winning/selling, then you should have no problems wrapping up the sale. Closing is just the natural end result of all the work you've already done.

I don't intend to compete with Tom Hopkins, the great sales trainer, or any of the other training pros on the subject of closing. They will tell you about the different types of closes to use, such as the alternative close: "Would you like red or blue?" "Delivery in three weeks or four?" Sure, there are a lot of methods for closing, and if you are leading an enterprise sales organization, every member of your team should have read or listened to one of the great trainers on closing.

When it comes to closing, some of the important aspects to keep in mind are:

- Listen for verbal clues that the prospect is ready to move forward with a transaction—what we call "buying signals".

- When you hear buying signals, offer a trial close. A trial close is a test question to determine if the prospect is ready. For instance, "How soon would you like to schedule installation?" "What color do you prefer?"

- It is said to ABC (always be closing), however, in my opinion if you try to close too early you lose credibility with the prospect and they move away. Be patient and let them move toward you. If you make yourself available and they really are interested, they will come to you.

- Use a closing technique that best fits your personal style. Don't try to imitate someone else, or you'll likely come off as unnatural and awkward. For instance, if you are more consultative by nature, then use a consultative closing technique. "Based on the information you have shared with me about your project to date, the optimal solution I recommend is xyz. Do you agree, and if so, when would you like to get started?"

- Know your close plan. Know who is going to do what to whom to result in your receipt of a valid order. In large companies, this is a signed contract and a purchase order.

- Always try to get a firm payment obligation. For instance, don't close blanket orders that contain no upfront transaction/payment obligation.

- When you ask for the order, don't say another word until you get an answer.

- Once you gain agreement and close, wrap up and leave as quickly as possible.

- Never go out to lunch or dinner immediately following a close. Schedule your thank you lunch a few weeks later. Too many closed deals have come undone at early celebrations.

Chapter 10

THE PROBLEM WITH CORE SKILLS

What's the main problem with core selling skills? Not enough sales professionals are proficient in all of them. The reason? I would say that the lack of complete proficiency in core selling skills boils down to insufficient professional sales training.

I suspect that many of the newer sales professionals in the market place may never have had the benefit of reading or going through training on closing or the other core skills. In the old days, we went through extensive training courses. We were videotaped and reviewed on our basic sales skills. Major companies like IBM, XEROX, DEC, NCR, and HP were all famous for providing excellent basic sales training. People who went through those trainings were fully grounded in all the core selling skills.

That was then. Today, many of those who were so well–trained have moved on to other careers or into management. Meanwhile, the next generations have not received the same level of investment into their sales competencies, and this is my primary issue with enterprise sales today. Without real training, it is no surprise that our enterprise sales professionals are falling short.

I'm not a trainer, so I'm not trying to inject new spending into my own market. What I care about is improving the quality of work in my profession. After 22 years, I've grown sick of seeing the game played poorly when, with some investment in training and a bit of effort by the individual, the level of play could improve significantly. In the recent past, we were all spoiled by the successes of industries requiring enterprise sales. Demand and buying trends have insulated us and prevented the exposure of our profession's growing weakness. Or have they?

Let's look at the 900 small companies I mentioned before—the ones with $10 million or less in annual sales. What's preventing them from breaking out and growing further? I'm sure their products or services are compelling at some level. I doubt they can charge premium prices at this stage, but still some of them have reached $10 million in sales. The problem, and I would bet on this, is lack of consistency across all of their *sales professionals*. Why am I so certain? It's like this:

To begin with, when a small company loses an opportunity they have spent a good amount of time pursuing, it has a much greater impact on them than it would have on a large company. The opportunity cost alone is much greater. So, based on what I've seen, I would speculate that in most of those small companies there is one real, quality sales professional, maybe two, and sometimes it is the CEO or maybe a seasoned sales veteran. The issue then becomes one of scale. All CEOs have a pretty busy job, especially start–up CEOs. Remember enterprise sales is *complex sales*, which involves navigating and soliciting a hierarchy of several individuals on the buyer's side in a way that influences the prospect to do business with you and not with your competitor. Think that can be done with an occasional meeting or two? Think it can be done by one, or at most two, sales professionals who often have other roles or jobs to attend to? Think again.

On the other hand, what if one of these small companies had ten or twenty of the highest caliber sales professionals? What if they were all well–trained and highly proficient? What if each demonstrated a high degree of proficiency in core selling skills? Let's do some rough calculations. Twenty reps times, say $3 million in annual sales... that equals $60 million in sales. You can twist the numbers and play with different scenarios, but the point is simple. It comes down to scale and competency. Easy for me to say, but unfortunately, it's not all that easy to accomplish, as we will see in our next chapter. Once you have the right people, they need to be managed in a way that drives highest degree of operational execution. Once you get your competent sales professionals, you need equally competent managers.

Chapter 11

MANAGEMENT TRAINING

While, as I have pointed out already, there is a woeful lack of investment in professional training for sales reps, there hasn't been a heck of a lot of attention paid to training sales leaders either. Here's the typical scenario: After achieving success in sales as well as demonstrating leadership traits, a sales rep may be promoted and become a sales leader. However, in many cases very little, if any, leadership training is provided, and as a consequence, newly promoted sales leaders aren't prepared to perform effectively in many of the important aspects of a sales leader's role. The most important in my opinion is effective coaching.

I experienced this first hand while I was with a very large software company. I had completed three successful years in direct sales, including receiving the Global Account Manager of the Year Award from the Executive Committee. Afterward my area VP offered me a double promotion to regional manager. So far everything was great until I received the largest quota in my VP's area applied to the least lucrative region at the time. I received no training in sales leadership, or any leadership for that matter. I also never received any coaching. The area VP was a likeable person, but way too hands–off. I needed management level training and I did not get it. What training I got came from the school of hard knocks.

I've learned a great deal since then. Later in this section I discuss the leadership training I received while at another company, but for now I want to look at what I have come to believe about hiring leaders. Based on my experience, when it comes to hiring sales leaders I believe the following attributes are the most desirable.

- Strong focus on achieving objectives
- Extroverted/Customer centric

- Down to earth, approachable
- Love of coaching/teaching
- Disciplined
- Ability to unify and bring people together for a common goal
- Results oriented
- Recognition oriented
- Enthusiastic
- Ability to entertain customers
- Passionate

COMMON CHARACTERISTICS OF SALES LEADERS

Throughout my career, I have also encountered other sales leaders with the following array of characteristics. While each has both pros and cons related to leading a sales organization, I suggest, whenever possible, avoiding people with these profiles in your leadership ranks... names withheld to protect the innocent.

Note: The following list is slightly tongue–in–cheek, but even where there's humor, there's a kernel of truth.

THE DEN FATHER OR MOTHER

Pros

- Beloved by every staff member
- Deep relationships with staff
- High on recognition
- Nurturing
- Supportive
- Comical
- Super friendly
- Super supportive

Cons

- Supports, rather than directs, when direct action is required.
- Noncommittal
- Lacks edge, and ability to make tough decisions
- Hires for personality, not necessarily ability

THE POLITICIAN

Pros

- Great for morale
- Well liked by everyone except direct manager
- Fun at meetings and parties
- Great joke teller and back slapper
- Upbeat
- High on recognition
- Broad relationships

Cons

- Time wasted on political "activism" and stroking others not spent on performing
- Missed results compensated for by BS smoke screens and political lobbying
- Disloyal/Prone to back–stabbing
- Not willing to take a stance
- Lacks edge and ability to make tough decisions
- Too risk averse
- Too internally focused vs. customer focused

THE ROOKIE

Pros

- Enthusiastic
- Passionate
- Hard working
- Customer focused
- Loves to sell

Cons

- Lacks management experience
- High on frustration
- Low on coaching
- Complainer

THE GENERAL

Pros

- Passionate
- Driven
- Ruthless competitor
- Externally focused
- Gets results

Cons

- Scares people
- Too intense
- High attrition rate
- Can't relate to non–performers

THE GODFATHER

Pros

- Passionate

- Committed
- Gets Results
- Manages Up Well

Cons

- Too much drama
- Threatens
- Yells

THE PLAYBOY

Pros

- Generates interesting stories

Cons

- A sexual harassment nightmare
- Too busy courting to manage

THE PARTY ANIMAL

Pros

- Throws awesome parties
- Also, generates interesting stories
- Makes everyone else look like a rock star on forecast calls and reviews
- Well liked by certain types of staff members

Cons

- Just one... Hands–off management approach, combined with frequent substance abuse, results in complete failure in every aspect of sales management.

Napoleonic

Pros

- Produces Results
- Gets Action
- Productive Staff
- Micro Manages

Cons

- Low Morale
- High attrition
- Not well liked
- High on drama

The Techie

Pros

- High on coaching and teaching
- Supportive on issues
- Strong technical aptitude can assist staff on presales items

Cons

- Usually lost in a sales leader's role
- Can't understand why customers don't behave more logically
- Can't understand why our technology was not chosen
- More comfortable in technical conversations
- Not great at connecting with customers
- Not strong at sales strategy

The Football Star

Pros

- Strong morale builder
- Team oriented

- Fired–up
- Gets the job done
- Competitive

Cons

- Not supportive. Expects people to figure things out on their own.
- Spends a lot of time in the gym.
- Can be dangerous at parties.
- Hide the women

THE PROFESSOR

Pros

- Strong on strategy
- Sick smart
- Gains respect as a thinker

Cons

- Not well liked
- Individualist
- Too into theory
- Not externally focused enough

THE EX–MILITARY OFFICER

Pros

- Great image
- Good communicator
- Confident
- Motivational
- Supportive

Cons

- Autocratic
- Rigid

- Risk Averse
- Political

THE GOLFER

Pros

- Great image
- Low handicap
- Great customer golf host

Cons

- Never available
- No support
- Usually fails

As you can see from the above lists of characteristics, I have experienced a variety of types of sales leaders. Indeed, variety is the spice of life, but we must be certain that we don't fall for sales leaders who just look the part but lack the attributes to get the job done. Our sales managers must also have a sufficient training resume and we must continue to invest in more training for them. If we want to resolve the crisis, we need to stop the cycle of hiring the wrong sales managers, throwing them against the wall and hoping they stick, and firing them few quarters later, only to start the cycle over again

Part III

Operational Execution

Chapter 12

OPERATIONAL EXECUTION

The link between a sales organization and operational execution should be obvious, but apparently it is not. Just mention "operational execution" in a group of sales professionals—and even among many sales leaders—and watch their faces. You're likely to see concern, nervousness, and even fear, in their eyes. You'd think you had just asked them to engage in a discussion of quantum mechanics or exo–biological morphologies. You've got to wonder why, don't you? Aren't enterprise sales executives part of a business function that has a strategic objective, distinct goals, and distinct key performance indicators that one can monitor to manage the operation? Do best practices exist, which can be scaled across a sales organization? Yes and yes. Strong operational execution is required in sales, just as it is in all other functions of a company.

So what's the issue? What's so nerve–wracking about operational execution? I think I know the answer, and it comes down to how people perceive sales—as an art or as a science. You often hear people talk about the "art of sales," but less often, "the science of sales." So many sales professionals and sales executives view themselves as artists, and so do many people outside the field.

I told you at the beginning of this book that I would address this issue. And so I will.

I know personally that this debate has been going on for at least the past two decades, since that is how long I have been hearing it discussed. Both arguments have merit, and I'd agree that sales is both an art and a science, but here's the gotcha! I believe that enterprise sales is more science than art. If you treat enterprise sales as merely an art, you will fail. A bold statement? Indeed, it is. And I'll say it again. You will fail.

Here's how I see it: If you treat enterprise sales exclusively from a science perspective, I don't think you will necessarily fail, however, neither do I think you will have the best sales talent in your organization. Without understanding the science perspective, however, you won't have any success, because enterprise sales requires a scientific approach—which is where operational execution comes in—along with a healthy dose of art.

Before we drill down further into operational execution, I'll elaborate somewhat on the issue of sales as art versus sales as science, and hopefully, by the time I'm done, you'll see where I'm coming from.

First, let's define our terms: "art" and "science". A quick search in the world's free encyclopedia, Wikipedia, returns the following description of art.

> "The term art is used to describe a particular type of creative production generated by human beings, and the term usually implies some degree of aesthetic value. An artist makes a work of art for various purposes, such as creating an experience for others or as part of a ritual. There is no general agreed–upon definition of art, since defining the boundaries of "art" is subjective, but the impetus for art is often called human creativity.
>
> Art is that which is made with the intention of stimulating the human senses as well as the human mind and or spirit. An artwork is normally assessed in quality by the amount of stimulation it brings about. The impact it has on people, the number of people that can relate to it, the degree of their appreciation, and the effect or influence it has or has had in the past, and all accumulate to the 'degree of art.' Most artworks that are widely considered to be "masterpieces" possess these attributes.
>
> Something is not generally considered 'art' when it stimulates only the senses, or only the mind, or when it has a different primary purpose than doing so. However, some contemporary art challenges this idea."

This definition of art attempts to describe the purpose of art, but falls intentionally short of actually defining the term by saying that there is "no general agreed–upon definition of art". Certainly, it's about creativity and aesthetics. And, again according to the Wikipedia, it's ultimately subjective, which is defined in The American Heritage Dictionary as "proceeding from or taking place within an individual's mind and unaffected by the outside world."

It's sometimes encouraging to think that we can put art into business, but how can we run a business without boundaries? How do we conduct business from a subjective viewpoint without being realistic about the outside world? Can our approach to sales only be based on individual creativity? I would say that the answer to these questions is no, particularly in an endeavor as complex as enterprise sales.

One way I look at art is that it is primarily created by an individual or a small group of individuals and can be enjoyed by others. The way I see enterprise sales is something quite different. Enterprise sales requires teamwork, boundaries, constant monitoring, interaction with external events, and a lot of hard, real–world objectivity. It sounds like our "artists" require some organization to help them. The organization that helps them also helps us accomplish our goal of increasing share holder value. It helps us by winning and keeping happy customers who provide us with revenue and profits.

I've known many enterprise sales "artists" in my day, and many of them were very good at selling. However, I also noticed that they were even better when their manager helped them by creating some, but not too much, process to fully leverage their talents. It's the right amount of artistry and the right amount of science that creates the formula for success. Of course we are talking about management science not chemistry.

Let's go back to the Wikipedia again and look at the definition of management science:

> "Management science, or MS, is the discipline of using mathematics, and other analytical methods, to help make better business decisions. While often considered synonymous with Operations research (OR), MS is differentiated by being generally thought to have a more practical, rather than academic, bent.
>
> Some of the fields within Management Science include: decision analysis, optimization, simulation, forecasting, game theory, net-

work/transportation forecasting models, mathematical modeling, data mining, probability and statistics, Morphological analysis, resources allocation, project management as well as many others.

The management scientist's mandate is to use rational, systematic, science–based techniques to inform and improve decisions of all kinds. Of course, the techniques of management science are not restricted to business applications but may be applied to military, medical, public administration, charitable groups, political groups or community groups.

MS is also concerned with so–called"soft–operational analysis", which concerns methods for strategic planning, strategic decision support, and Problem Structuring Methods (PSM). At this level of abstraction, mathematical modeling and simulation will not suffice. Therefore, during the past 30 years, a number of non–quantified modeling methods have been developed. These include morphological analysis and various forms of Influence Diagrams."

As a business leader, I like this definition. It talks rational… systematic… making informed decisions based on analysis. To my disappointment, a lot of sales leaders and reps I've worked with in the past didn't seem to be that interested in the management science aspect of the business. Why is that? Perhaps it is because no one ever explained to them how MS could be applied in a sales environment and how it could benefit their performance and the performance of the organization. Or maybe it's just that they were afraid of something…

The biggest fear of many professionals, and especially sales professionals, is being "micromanaged". I don't think this term requires any definition. And for some sales professionals, MS approaches can be perceived as micromanagement. Certainly, the significant increase in visibility and monitoring of key performance indicators in sales environments may tend to add to such concerns. However, in my own work I have demonstrated how one can apply MS in an enterprise sales organization to drive strong operational execution, and to do so in a way that empowers sales professionals and their managers, without producing a micromanagement culture. It is actually pretty basic, but it requires a shift to hands–on coaching.

Shifting to a culture of hands–on coaching isn't easy, because so many sales leaders who have attempted to do so have done it poorly. When they were hands–on, they micromanaged, creating a negative result and producing a fear of leaders who take such hands–on approaches. Of course, in contrast, many sales leaders are totally hands–off, which creates a different set of issues. I'll discuss that situation and how to improve it a bit later. First, let's look at how a bit of management science could be applied in various areas of an enterprise sales operation to help us out of the current crisis, as it relates to operational execution.

Most large companies have their "blessed" CRM system or, to all intents and purposes, their "sacred" Sales Methodology, and I suspect that most non–sales leaders think that these are the equivalent of operational execution. At best, these many types of CRM systems are information warehouses. Their sales methodologies are attempts to create a recipe for a successful sales cycle, not sales organization.

What about our CRM system, then? Doesn't that do the trick? Not exactly. A lot of companies hire consultants and pay them a ton of money to establish CRM, but that's not what I'm talking about. I would bet a large sum of money that most companies do not have a framework to drive the operational execution of their sales organization. Sure, they have a sales methodology and a forecasting system. They probably also have a customer relationship management system where the reps store their leads and contacts, get prompted for follow up action, create opportunities, document their opportunity strategy, and so forth.

So the question is, how on earth do these systems facilitate the necessary interaction between player and coach? The answer is, they don't! You might ask, What about all the reports we can run? What about all the great data we have access to? I am putting a stake in the ground and stating that CRM systems are too general. So what if you have zillions of data points about your customers? It's just data until it's organized as key performance indicators and used in coaching. That's why I'm saying that performance management coaching is a critical, but missing, aspect.

Chapter 13

MANAGEMENT SCIENCE AND
SUCCESS PLANNING

Let's look at each area of operational execution for an enterprise sales organization, why it is an area of crisis, and, in brief, how management science can be used to improve operational execution in enterprise sales organizations.

Lack of execution is at the heart of most business issues related to enterprise sales, and I want to look at how management science can be applied to improve the operational aspects of an enterprise sales environment. First, let's look at the symptoms of poor execution. If you have any of the following, you can make a good guess why you also have poor sales execution by both sales leaders and individual contributors:

- Poor Forecast Visibility
- Lack of Forecast Accuracy
- High Loss Rate
- Inferior Pipeline Size
- Small Deal Sizes
- Inconsistent Revenue Goal Attainment
- Lack of Balanced Performance Across Quarters

This list could be considerably longer, but you probably know where I'm going with this. Let's dig a little deeper into the problem—the crisis in the enterprise.

"HANDS–OFF" SALES MANAGEMENT:

If your sales leadership philosophy is "hands–off," then I'm sorry to say, you are part of the problem and not part of the solution. Let's look at what I mean by the distinction between "hands–off" and "hands–on". It's a lousy metaphor, primarily because it reeks of micromanagement. However, I've always viewed it as "hands on" the business, "hands on" the game, NOT "hands on" the players. What I mean here is that "hands on" the business/game is when the leader is watching the game closely, helping players who need help, supporting players who do not, and making adjustments to the game plan as quickly as the conditions change, and the need for change arises. That's not personal micromanagement, it's participation in success.

In my opinion an effective enterprise sales leader stays connected with all aspects of his or her business, i.e. pipeline numbers, forecasts, performance of middle management sales leaders, performance of reps, account activity, strategic opportunities, sales call volume, and so forth. The list is endless, but that's what the game is all about.

The captain of any ship spends most of his/her time on or around the bridge, watching over the operation of the ship. Great captains also know the pulse of the crew and command their loyalty and respect. This type of support doesn't come from hanging out in your cabin, planning the next great cruise around the world. It means being engaged and connected with the entire ship, knowing what is going on, and being ready to act for the good of the entire voyage and everyone onboard.

Metaphorically, sales leaders need to be like the good captain—they need to be in the game. They need to be out visiting their customers, observing firsthand the play of their teams, market conditions and many other external factors. Additionally, effective senior level enterprise sales leaders need to be completely engaged while staying very close to their direct reports.

This may all seem very basic to you. You might be thinking, Aren't all sales leaders like this? Frankly, the answer is no, they are not. In the technology sector, where I have worked for more than two decades, the market and customer buying patterns are very dynamic. The cliché joke is that we age in dog years for each year we spend in technology, and I wonder if there isn't some truth to it, based on my own experience.

This may seem like an odd segue, but bear with me. It makes a point… When I interview a sales leader candidate and they are visibly very tan, I may have the following conversation:

"How it is possible to maintain a tan like that in our industry?" I ask.

Quite often the answer is, "I am an avid golfer."

"That's great," I reply. "What's your handicap?"

"My handicap is a 2."

"Wow, that's awesome. How often do you play golf?"

At this point, the candidate may begin to realize that there's a purpose to my questioning. Maintaining a nice tan and a 2 handicap on the links is all fine and good, and I have nothing against Jack Welch, who famously stated that leaders should have the best direct reports in the world so they can maintain a great golf handicap and play often, BUT this dog does not hunt in the enterprise sales world.

I have seen many sales managers who spend a ton of time out of the office, but not in front of customers or their people, and they tend to be very well liked by the nonperforming members of their staff because they are completely hands–off. At the same time they are resented by the high performers for never being around to assist or support them, while they are banging out consistent 50–hour weeks, quarter after quarter. Don't get me wrong. I'm not suggesting that we ask sales professionals at any level to punch a clock. I'm just stating that the closer a sales leader is to their business, the higher the probability for success , the tighter the ship and the better the real performers will do.

The other crisis point is that sales leaders who are "hands–on" often create conflict by doing "hands–on" in the negative sense of the expression. By doing so, they create an environment of unhealthy conflict, and anyone in business knows that unhealthy conflict is counterproductive. So you might ask, Are you saying there's such a thing as "healthy" conflict? Absolutely! Any HR pro will tell you that the problem isn't conflict. The problem is how conflict is managed. And if conflict is mismanaged, it can snowball out of control, like when a sales leader shies away from discussions over missed numbers to avoid conflict.

So where does management science come into this discussion of leadership styles and conflict? Well, I have a pretty healthy respect for management science, as I can illustrate by how I used it in my last job to move an organization away from negative conflict into positive results.

I knew going into the job that all was not well. My first clue was that I was interviewing in secret locations. Without going into all the gory details, the executive vice president was a strong leader, but the leadership below him, while perfectly likeable professionals, were not making the numbers. Out of professional courtesy, I am not going to go any further than that.

On my second day in the job, the top rep in our division came into my office and sat down. I could tell by the look on his face that he was not a happy camper. He asked me about my background and track record, and, after I briefed him, he asked me why I took this job. I was shocked at first, but, one after another, I had heard the same complaints from the rest of the team. They were not making their numbers. They were not making enough money. HQ did not support them. Marketing sucked. There were not enough leads, and so on.

I lived forty miles from my office , and on my drive home, I was very depressed; I had a realization that what I thought was a small turnaround, looked much bigger than I had anticipated. However, good things often come to us unexpectedly, and so I have to thank my daily commute for being one of those unexpectedly good things. While driving, with all these problems swirling in my head, I was able to take advantage of that "quality" alone time to think through the issues. When I reached my driveway, I felt much better.

I had come to the realization that I had a choice. I could continue to perpetuate the status quo, continuing the same "hands off" management approach that created a culture of complaints and excuses, or I could apply simple "hands on" management science techniques to fix the issues. Just as important as the approach was providing leadership that served as an advocate for the field and being an agent of cultural change to establish a high–performance organization, based on quarterly results and recognition.

Before making the changes I envisioned, however, to quote Jim Collin's *Good to Great*, I had to "confront the brutal facts" and get everyone else to do so as well. Once we acknowledged our current reality, we could take a disciplined thought and action approach to fix the business. I dug deeper in the issues, and this is the list of what I presented to my manager shortly after I joined the company:

ISSUES

- Lack of Revenue Goal Achievement
- Lack of Quota Achievement by Individual Contributors
- "Wallet Share" per Account is very low
- Reactive vs. Proactive Selling
- Lack of a Balanced Pipeline for Consistent Quarterly Achievement
- Insufficient Qualification
- Lack of Forecast Visibility
- Inaccurate Forecasting
- Low Direct Sales Call Volume
- Need to Shift from Product Feature Centric to Solution Centric
- Insufficient "C" Level Selling
- Insufficient Team Selling
- Not leveraging Senior Management with Prospects
- Lack of Cross Selling of Service Lines

- ¬ Average Sale Size too low
- ¬ Sales Communication Lacks Consistency
- ¬ Ability to deliver Executive Level "Pitch" needs improvement
- ¬ Confusing Selling vs. Installing
- ¬ Focus on Excuses and not Results
- ¬ Insufficient Alliance partnering
- ¬ No Close Planning
- ¬ Lack of Account Development

The list above is not unique. I hear from people in many other organizations who have the same issues. Certainly, many people in the tech industry will identify with some or most of the issues on the list above.

In my situation, I realized that we needed a framework that would enable the sales leaders to be more "hands–on" and more actively involved in the monitoring and management of their business. We also needed a framework that engaged the sales reps and empowered them to take responsibility for their own success metrics. Further, we needed a framework that enabled frequent, positive, coaching sessions that were fact based—in other words, objective and not emotionally charged. And for those frameworks, we utilized the area of management science known as performance management within our sales organizations.

My approach to the problem was something I had created at a prior company called Success Planning. The title was very important to me because I wanted to educate everyone involved with the framework that we were doing this to increase their chances of success, not to micromanage them. We were going to motivate everyone to take a daily view of how they were doing against their individual key performance indicators, and then roll those numbers upward to each director, to each VP, and then to me.

No longer were we going to hire reps and send them off with a quota, without coaching and supporting them. Enterprise sales professionals are knowledge workers and I believe that they should be treated as such. Human capital is precious and should not be treated as a disposable commodity. Commonly, managers hope for success without doing much to ensure it, then, when the reps fall below their quotas, they are put on a performance plan. Most reps never meet their performance plans, so they are ultimately terminated, and another human resource is wasted, I think needlessly. My goal was to manage our precious human capital for the highest probability of success all around, and behind this framework was the following set of actions we were going to take as leaders to address each of the issues.

- ¬ Larger Pipeline & Increased Close Rate
- ¬ Drive Sales Productivity and Balanced Performance
- ¬ C Level Prospecting & Cross–Selling
- ¬ Weekly Monitoring of Results
- ¬ Drive Prospecting Consistency
- ¬ Qualification Discipline
- ¬ Closer Management Scrutiny
- ¬ Push for Nine Sales Calls to Power Each Week
- ¬ Focus on Addressing Prospect's Acute Pain Points
- ¬ Sell Strategic Professional Services
- ¬ C Level Prospecting Campaign in Top 10 Accounts
- ¬ Hierarchical Selling
- ¬ Monitoring on a Weekly basis
- ¬ Management Scrutiny on Sales Activity
- ¬ Executive Pitch Training
- ¬ Attitude Adjustment
- ¬ Monitoring on a Weekly basis
- ¬ Drive Close Plans

If you are responsible for a sales organization, I highly recommend establishing Success Planning. You should see very strong results.

Chapter 14

Idea Flow/Cycle of Leadership

In my last job I had the privilege of participating in an executive training by Noel Tichy, a leading professor at the University of Michigan Business School, director of the school's Global Leadership Partnership, and a worldwide advisor to CEOs on leadership and transformation. Noel has written *The Cycle of Leadership*, and coauthored *The Leadership Engine and Control Your Destiny or Someone Else Will*.

Noel also set up Jack Welch's Croton Falls Management Training Program at GE, and he is a very effective teacher. I learned a tremendous amount about leadership from Noel. In particular, I took away two very important points:

1. Leaders need to invest the time to make sure everyone in their organization understands their teachable point of view, (where the leader is taking the organization).

2. An effective leader creates an environment where ideas and issues flow seamlessly from the bottom of the organization to the top. Noel calls this the "Upward Knowledge Spiral". The example of the opposite is the "all knowing" dictator who barks orders down through the organization, a leadership style that assures nobody will complain or raise issues, let alone offer ideas.

Noel's Upward Knowledge Spiral approach was consistent with what we were doing in our organization. Needless to say, I felt good to have that validation. However, this was not the case at prior companies, nor was it in the case when I first joined the current company. They held quarterly "Account Reviews," but I generally came away with the impression that the reviews were largely ineffective. After experiencing "death by PowerPoint" from each of the sales executives, as they offered their vast knowledge of their territory and accounts, I noticed that they only spent a little time on the numbers. Overall, their presentations were lacking depth and were poorly organized. Also, some of the presenters expressed ideas, suggestions, and complaints and some of them did not, but even when they did, I saw no disciplined approach to capturing and acting on the ideas, suggestions, and complaints.

When I assumed responsibility for the account reviews, I turned them into Quarterly Business Reviews. The first thing I did was ban PowerPoint. The rep's individual Success Plan Dashboards in Microsoft Excel would be the only format we would use, and, back to the main point, each QBR included a formal agenda space for issues and suggestions. Since the issues far outnumbered the suggestions, I introduced the concept of "Snake Hunting" into each Agenda, borrowing a term and approach from one of my self–adopted mentors, Ray Lane, senior partner at KPCB.

At first, my office kept the list and followed up with each functional area. However, keeping the list updated and organized got so overwhelming that our head of sales operations volunteered to take it over and track the items. At the end of the QBRs, the items were sent to each functional head, assigned out, acted on, and reported back, either at the next QBR, or sooner if the item had been resolved. The suggestions or ideas were shared at my manager's staff meetings with all functional heads and were used as input on our strategy. You can't get any more grass roots than that!

As good as I felt about our new procedures, and as validating as my classes had been, I still saw room for improvement. Noel's teachings served as a healthy reminder that the path to effective leadership is through a teachable point of view, ideas, values, and emotional energy/edge. I felt I had each one of these areas in my game, but that I could do a better job of balancing across all four and making sure my organization understood me as a leader and where we were going. In particular, I wasn't sure I was communicating my teachable point of view as effectively as I could with my direct reports and their directs. Taking a cue from the leadership class, I scheduled an all–hands meeting.

I'm a take–charge kind of person, so emotional energy/edge, or, as Noel defines it, the ability to make tough decisions quickly and the ability to exhibit high degrees of passion toward the business, were never an issue for me. I learned from Noel's class that I needed to make sure that my edge was balanced with openness, however.

Even though I always believed that everyone in my organization should be heard and recognized, and not just told what to do, I knew that was one area where I needed to pay close attention. I think this is a problem for some leaders who, though they know their business very well, may not always be as patient about listening to other ideas on how to get the job done, particularly when they know how it's been done effectively in the past. It's easy to think you've already seen every approach and discount new input, and it was very useful for me to reflect on this aspect of my leadership game and then apply it within my organization, to ensure that we were functioning at our best. It's all about the power of ideas and communication.

Performance Management Dashboards for Enterprise Sales

I searched in the online Webster's Encyclopedia on "performance management" and received the following Wikipedia description. Yes, that's right, Wikipedia. Anyway, let's take a look at an excerpted section of the entry*.

Performance Management Cycle

Performance management and improvement can be thought of as a cycle:

1. Performance Planning where goals and objectives are established

2. Performance Coaching where a manager intervenes to give feedback and adjust performance

3. Performance appraisal where individual performance is formally documented and feedback delivered

A performance problem is any gap between Desired Results and Actual Results. Performance improvement is any effort targeted at closing the gap between Actual Results and Desired Results.

* http://en.wikipedia.org/wiki/Performance_management

Business Performance Management (BPM) is a set of processes that help businesses discover efficient use of their business units, financial, human and material resources.

Source: adapted by the editor from Wikipedia, the free encyclopedia under a copy left GNU Free Documentation License (GFDL) from the article "Performance management."

I will confess that I am a big fan of using performance management. It is the most honest and straightforward way to manage. Once you agree with a person on the work that needs to get done, you provide advice and support along the way, and then assess and give feedback after evaluating the results.

I've worked at several companies in the past twenty–four years, and at every company, performance coaching was severely lacking or nonexistent within their sales organizations when I joined. In the last three of those companies, I was able to introduce performance management and implement it.

It seems so obvious. According to Wikipedia, there are three steps to the process, but it seems that only Steps 1 and 3—plan and appraise—are generally implemented. Why not Step 2—Coaching? In some cases, the problem may be due to personality differences, as I previously suggested. I believe there is another reason, however, and it's all about the frequency of evaluation. If you think about it, enterprise sales organizations generally make the mistake of looking at performance on an annual or a quarterly basis, instead of on a weekly, biweekly, or monthly basis. A year is a lifetime in enterprise sales, and a quarterly view provides you with only four performance management opportunities. What if you adopted a weekly, biweekly or monthly approach?

Specifically, what if each sales professional and manager up the line had a simple dashboard which stated quarterly goals and measured progress against these goals on a weekly basis—goals like total sales pipeline, total upside, total commit, total bookings, plus similar details for each product or service being sold. In enterprise sales, this data is considered to be among our most important key performance indicators. And, of course, we can also track sales call volume, calls to power and other useful metrics. It seems to me that the more frequently a team tracks their KPIs/progress in a discussion between the players and coaches, the better the odds for success. Twenty-six checkpoints between coaches and players make me feel a heck of a lot better than four checkpoints.

So why aren't weekly forecast calls or meetings great checkpoints? Most forecast calls focus on data that is in a forecast system and, in general, how someone is doing against quota. As such, the sales leader is acting in more of a reporting capacity than a coaching capacity. And frankly, it takes a lot of time to do a competent job forecasting. Performance coaching also requires time and specific attention. I don't believe you can do a good job at either if you try to do both of them at the same time.

CEOs should pay close attention to the following point: I believe in paying enterprise sales professionals very well and at the same time leading them to the highest possible level of productivity. There is a huge potential gain here over existing practices. Also, "legacy" sales leaders need to wake up to the fact that they may be allowing suboptimal performance in their organization if their management team is not tracking KPIs and providing performance coaching at least twice a month. Don't tell me it's being done, either, because I know for a fact that it's just lip service, and I can prove it very easily.

Here's a test you can use. Pick up the phone at different points in the quarter and contact some of your players and leaders. Ask each of them how they are doing. They will tell you they are doing great. Then ask them to tell you exactly how far away from their goal for the quarter they are, based on bookings up to that week. Some may know; many won't. Then ask them the same question concerning different product categories. If this is not a fair question for the reps, based on how you delegate goals, then ask the leaders, who surely will have goals by product. Ask them where they stand against the quarterly objective for Product A, B, and C. Also, ask them how often they engage with their manager for one-on-one formal performance coaching. I am certain their answers will prove my point, if they answer truthfully.

So, even when some of your management believes they have the situation under control, they really don't. Their methods do not adequately position their company for the greatest possible successes, yet they persist in using them. Why? Two reasons in my opinion: First, a lack of timely business data. Second, cultural resistance. Remember our examination of "hands-off" management? I think the same issue comes into play here.

I remember one particular time when I was in a leadership role, when I realized how badly we needed frequent performance coaching and monitoring. No one was focused on monitoring weekly or monthly achievement of success metrics, key performance indicators or sales achievement to date. Unfortunately, the data we needed was not available, and the company's culture had avoided obtaining it so we decided that we would get it done ourselves. I introduced performance coaching and, as I said previously, I called it Success Planning. I created a Success Planning dashboard format and an ongoing process of coaching off of the dashboards. Both the dashboards and the coaching were key elements in our turnaround strategy to make our numbers. I am convinced that the Success Planning ingredient played a major role in helping us reach or exceed our goals for 12 out of 14 quarters. The two quarters we missed were not surprises, either. Thanks to our frameworks, we knew we were at risk during those particular periods.

I will confess that it took awhile before my organization realized how beneficial the Success Planning methods were for everyone. At first, the reps complained about having to input the business data manually into their individual dashboards, which, by the way, consisted of two worksheets in Microsoft Excel. I was sensitive to their complaints, but what better way to get knowledge workers focused on their goals and progress than by having them personally working with their own data? The time sink they complained about consisted of about two hours at the beginning of the quarter to clean up all the data and organize it, and then about 30–60 minutes a week, maximum, to keep it up to date. Ultimately, we found ways to automate the process, which, of course, made it more effective and less of a pain.

A SUCCESS PLANNING EXAMPLE

Here is an example of a Success Plan. The two-page Microsoft Excel worksheet lays out the quantitative and qualitative goals for the sales professional for the quarter. It is a simple two dimensional view of how someone is performing against their goals. *See Figure 1 on page 92.*

Figure 1 shows the first worksheet, which is quantitative in nature. It displays listing of a sales professional's opportunities for the current quarter by the stage of progression down the sales funnel. The Success Plan owner can see the total value of the opportunities they are working by product type and in total, compared to their quota for the quarter. Thus, they keep a running tab of the delta between their sales actuals and their sales quota. The report shows if their opportunities are progressing in line with the passing of time in the quarter. It also shows if they are cross-selling sufficiently. Total pipeline is listed at the bottom and uses a 3X factor as the benchmark. *See Figure 2 on page 93.*

The second example is more qualitative in nature. It lists the areas of performance management that a manager would be interested in tracking and coaching—qualitative goals such as C-level education, named account penetration, new calls to power, total sales call volume, etc.

Is this "micromanagement"? I suppose it depends on your definition and the connotation you give to the term. To me, it simply offers a means by which to establish fair goals, monitor the attainment of those goals, and provide performance coaching before there is a performance problem. I have seen and proven the effectiveness of this approach. Sadly, in my experience, the only individuals who resist this type of approach are individuals who are lost and do not wish to be found. You may have seen this type of sales rep. They are tickled pink with their base salary alone.

I have found that performance coaching is much more effective when the individual's success plan is the basis for the discussion. Rather than dealing strictly at an emotional level, which is often common in one-on-one meetings among sales professionals, a manager can have a "fact-based" conversation with their staff member. Enterprise sales organiza-

#	A	B	C	D
1	Success Plan Roadmap			
2	1. Closed and Booked Opportunities:	Quarter	Total	Product A
3	Account / Opportunty Name			
4				
5				
6	Sub Total Closed and Booked Opportunities		$0	$0
7	Total Quota		$1,000,000	
8	Less			
9	(+) = Achieve or Exceed Quota. (-) = Quota Shortfall		-1,000,000	
10	percentage of quota:		0%	0%
11	2. Committed Opportunities (Always included in the Forecast)	Quarter	Total	Product A
12	Account / Opportunty Name			
13				
14	Sub Total Committed Opportunities		$0	$0
15	Subtotal Committed and Booked		$0	$0
16	Total Quota		$1,000,000	
17	Less			
18	(+) = Achieve or Exceed Quota. (-) = Quota Shortfall		-1,000,000	
19	percentage of quota:		0%	0%
20	3. Qualified Upside Opportunities (Can be included in the Forecast if feasible)	Quarter	Total	Product A
21	Account / Opportunty Name			
22				
23	Sub Total Qualified Opportunities		$0	$0
24	Plus Booked & Committed Business		$0	$0
25	Sub Total Booked, Committed & Qualified Opportunities		$0	$0
26	Total Quota		$1,000,000	
27	Less			
28	(+) = Achieve or Exceed Quota. (-) = Quota Shortfall		-$1,000,000	
29	percentage of quota:		0%	0%
30	4. Unqualified Upside Opportunities (Not to be included in the Forecast)	Quarter	Total	Product A
31	Account / Opportunty Name			
32				
33				
34				
35	Sub Total UnQualified Upside Opportunities		$0	$0
36	Total Pipeline = Booked, Committed, Qualified & UnQualified Upside Business		$0	$0
37	percentage of quota:		0%	0%
38	Total Pipeline for the Quarter		$0	$0
39	1/3 Pipeline		$0	$0

Figure 1: Success Planning Worksheet 1

List Key Performance Indicators and Other Success Metrics for Performance Coaching and Review

	A	B	C
1	List Key Performance Indicators and Other Success Metrics for Performance Coaching and Review		
2			
3	1. Priority Accounts for Cross Selling	First Department	Second Department
4			
5			
6			
7			
8			
9			
10	2. Weekly Sales Call Volume	# of Calls to Power Past Week	Name & Title
11			
12			
13			
14			
15			
16			
17			
18	3. C Level Education / Relationship Building	Name / Status of C Level Relationship	Date of Last Meeting
19			
20			
21			
22			
23	4. Product Demonstration Activity	# of Demos	Audience
24			
25			
26			
27			
28			
29	5. Hierarchical Selling on Enterprise Opportunities	Updates on Sales Strategy	Detailed Close Plan in place?
30	List Opportunity A		

Figure 2: Success Planning Worksheet 2

tions can dramatically increase the performance of their sales organizations simply by adopting the practice of regularly scheduled one-on-one performance coaching sessions based on performance metrics/goals. When more attention and collaboration occurs between sales management and sales representatives, the performance of the entire organization increases.

There are still other reasons why performance coaching can improve macro-level issues in enterprise sales. For instance, another important reason why I see enterprise sales in a state of crisis is how widespread the complaints are about the effectiveness—or lack of effectiveness—of sales organizations. Almost every top sales leader, CEO, or executive I speak with complains about the lack of his or her sales organization's ability to cross-sell multiple products or services, to provide sufficient visibility into their forecast, to forecast accurately, to manage opportunities well, to plan effective strategies to penetrate accounts…. I can go on with this list, but I have to pause here. I find myself wondering, after all the money that has been spent in the past ten years on expensive CRM systems, management consultants, and the like, how can this be? What I was listing above are some of the core deliverables in sales, yet small, medium and large companies are all struggling with these issues. How can this be, and what the heck is going on?

I'm afraid the truth is that, while many leaders acknowledge that sales professionals have different and specific attributes, not many people truly understand the unique attributes and characteristics of an enterprise sales force. Therefore, a false assumption is made that sales will just get the job done, and when they do they get paid, and when they don't they get fired. I hope that by my putting this thought down in black and white, you can see how naïve this view can be.

I found a promising example of how the consulting firm McKinsey helped one company use coaching to retool their sales force. The article is titled, "Rapid Transformation of a Sales Force". (AUGUST 2008 by Josh Leibowitz and Ben Vonwiller). In the article, the authors state:

> "To ensure that these changes endured, the company instituted recurring structured-coaching sessions where area managers used the performance tools to evaluate sales managers and to pinpoint and

address their weaknesses. The sales managers in turn coached their reps in the same way. Both the tools and the coaching sessions played a crucial role in the success of the program, which was implemented in most markets within the required six months. By the end of a year, the unit had increased its lead conversion rates by 20 percent and the number of self-generated leads by 25 percent."*

In the following chapters, we'll look at cross-selling and sales forecasting, two additional crisis points that Success Planning can resolve:

* http://www.mckinseyquarterly.com/Transforming_a_large_and_distributed_sales_force_2178

Chapter 15

CROSS–SELLING

Most folks are aware that cross–selling means selling multiple products or services to the same customer. It can be done on a first sale, but is usually done on subsequent sales. This is so straightforward that you have to wonder why it's a crisis point?

It seems to me that ineffective cross–selling is really one of the growing pains a company experiences as it increases in size and age. Most companies emerge successfully from conception with a single product or service to sell. As the company learns from their customers, new product ideas emerge from perceived market needs. Additional products are added to drive new revenue streams and so on. At some point, the CEO probably has had a conversation with the company's sales leader, asking how to best stimulate the sales of the new products. That sales leader probably convinced the CEO to provide a "carrot" and not a "stick," thus offering higher commission rates for the new products, rather than issue product–specific quotas and monitor performance closely. The common cliché response in enterprise sales is, "A dollar is a dollar," which negates the importance of the value of cross–selling.

To be fair to most sales reps and leaders, they have probably been burned in the past by a new product that fell flat on its face in the market, not reaching that twenty million in sales right out of the gate, as the CEO evangelized it. So, to reduce risk, the sales leader convinces the CEO just to pay more money for new product sales. Of course what they fail to realize is that most enterprise sales representatives who have installed–base customers are scared to death to risk screwing up their current revenue stream from the existing product or products by introducing a new and untested product. This is why I believe, in most cases, that the "carrot" approach fails to meet plan. It's an approach that empowers sales professionals to decide if they want to follow through on implementing the strategic plan. Yes, you heard me correctly. You are giving your sales force the ability to decide not to sell additional products.

As a sales leader, I was accustomed to carrying product–specific quotas and being held accountable for making them. So why would I not want the sales reps in my organization to be aligned with my goals? What is the downside? Frankly, I don't see one. I'm not against paying additional incentives, or "carrots," to sell new products but please don't forget the accountability factors i.e. quotas.

Further, if everyone below the head of sales thinks a "dollar is a dollar," then who is going to monitor and coach sales professionals to cross–sell? See the point? The answer is, no one. I actually had an area VP of sales in my organization admit to me that he was not guiding his reps to cross–sell, and that they had an "any sale works" attitude. Man! How do you think the GMs and product managers would feel about that?

Of course, solving this problem can be very straightforward:

1. Establish performance coaching between the sales managers and reps on a biweekly basis.
2. Include tracking sales by product/cross–selling as part of the dashboard or Success Plan document used in the performance coaching.
3. Set product specific targets at every level in field sales.
4. Pay additional percentage points for sales of the product(s) you want cross–sold.
5. Establish a cross–selling quota attainment rule as a hurdle for earning President's Club. You can set the rule to fit your business scenario, i.e. achieve quota for two or more products or three or more products, or all products, etc.
6. Make sure your sales force has had adequate sales training to sell the additional products, not just product training, but the sales end of the training as well.

That's it. If you want to fix your cross–selling problem, take the steps above.

Chapter 16

SALES FORECASTING

One of the most critical capabilities within any company is the ability to project future revenue and expense accurately. Since most revenue is based on sales bookings, accurate sales forecasting is a critical success factor for most companies. Forecast accuracy is often assigned as a qualitative goal of sales leaders and sometimes sales representatives. If this is the case, then why do we often hear on earnings calls that "we" came up short on our forecasts due to some macro–level economic or micro–level operational issue? While some companies have an excellent track record of meeting Wall Street's expectations, many do not.

During the past twenty–two years, I have yet to hear any senior executive say they were very happy with sales forecast accuracy and visibility. This is odd, considering that we spend money on expensive forecasting systems, which are often part of even more expensive customer relationship management (CRM) systems.

So what's the crisis point here? Simply put, it's that enterprise sales forecasts often lack accuracy and predictability. They are also not visible enough to the senior leadership team. And, although this is no small matter of frustration inside many corporations, for obvious reasons it never gets exposed to the public.

We can see the problem. That's not so hard. Now, let's look at the root causes. It starts with core skills. Do you remember when we talked about issues within the core skills of prospecting, qualifying, presenting, negotiating, and closing? Well, skilled and accurate forecasting is a major concern as well. Many sales reps and managers I have encountered throughout my career lack the ability to communicate meaningful forecast information accurately and efficiently. Sales leaders have to spend far too much time trying to extract the status and next steps of a sales cycle. Obtaining accurate forecast predictions for a particular quarter is also very challenging.

I believe this issue can be resolved through training and adherence to discipline throughout the organization.

Let's all start on the same page, by defining our terms. To help with that, I'm providing this mini–glossary of Sales 101 terms. These terms represent the baseline of knowledge needed to train your organization on enterprise sales forecasting.

Forecast—A report communicating the total pipeline of opportunities, the level of qualification of each opportunity, the current stage of a sales cycle, the value of the opportunity, the sale quantity, the anticipated close date, the product type, the responsible parties, the name of the account, the name of the project, etc.

Close Date—The anticipated date for closing the sale

Start Date—The date the opportunity was first forecasted.

Owner—The assigned sales representative

Product—What is being sold?

Quantity—How much is being sold

Value—Dollar amount being sold

Stage—Current stage in the sales cycle

Qualification Levels—Lead, unqualified opportunity, qualified opportunity, commit, closed, booked.

Suspect—A stranger we assume may have interest.

Prospect—Someone we have spoken with or met and have determined some interest exists.

Cold Lead—The name and contact information of a suspect.

Warm Lead—The name and contact information of a qualified prospect.

Hot Lead—The name and contact information of a qualified prospect or customer with an immediate need.

Qualification—A set of criteria used to determine the size, timing, and whether an opportunity is real or not.

Filter—The level of qualification of an opportunity e.g. pain, fit, value, power, plan

Pain—The level of business pain that exists in the project or organization you are qualifying

Fit—The degree to which your product or service fits within the customer's business or technical environment

Value—The business value your product or service delivers

Power—The level of power, influence, and importance your prospect or customer wields in his or her organization.

Plan—The customer's buying plan—timeframe, spend amount, etc.

Unqualified Upside—A lead that has been initially qualified opportunity, but has not yet been fully qualified.

Qualified Upside—An opportunity that has been fully opportunity qualified for pain, fit, value, power, and plan.

Win Rate—The percentage of sales wins vs. losses

ASP—Average Sales Price

Close Rate—The number of sales closed within a certain period of time.

Sales Funnel or Sales Pipeline—The total value of all opportunities in a forecast report.

Quarterly Forecast—The amount of booked, closed, committed, and forecasted upside expected to close within a quarter.

Slipped—A forecasted item which did not close on the forecasted date.

Booked Opportunity—A closed sale which completed the order entry process and received an assigned order number.

Closed Opportunity—Receipt of a signed contract and purchase order.

Committed Opportunity—An opportunity which a sales representative has flagged as having the highest probability of closing. Typically reaches this point after a verbal commit or award from a customer.

However, the timing of the sale may still be up in the air if not further qualified at this point.

Upside—One of the most ambiguous terms used in sales forecasting, perhaps intentionally. A common definition of upside is everything else that is not booked, closed, or committed. (Statistical sales forecasters love to apply probability of closing percentages against this area, a practice that doesn't actually work in reality.)

Let's get back to the crisis point. Over the years, I have come into contact with many sales organizations, sometimes as a consultant, sometimes helping my employer with due diligence—evaluating the sales organizations of companies my company was considering purchasing—and often through my work experience in either interviewing or working together with sales professionals. And through it all, I've consistently found that a significant number of the people I've encountered simply lacked structure and discipline with regard to their sales forecasts. Looked at from a different perspective, forecasting is another form of financial reporting and, frankly for good reasons, not many sales professionals get turned on by financial reporting.

Where have I found the area most lacking in forecast discipline? In the upside category. If you want to increase the accuracy of your forecast dramatically, pay attention to this next part: To achieve an accurate quarterly forecast, start dividing upside into two categories.—fully qualified upside or unqualified upside. What's the difference? Look at it in terms of the current quarter. It is either fully qualified upside, or it isn't. And if it is not, then it should be called unqualified upside, and treated as such.

Let's look a little more deeply at the concepts of fully and unqualified upsides.

Qualified Upside—A fully qualified opportunity for the current quarter where pain has been identified, fit has been determined, there is compelling value for our offering, all applicable levels of power are engaged and have planned to purchase this quarter (not necessarily from us, or it should probably be a commit item).

Unqualified Upside—An opportunity that is assessed after a sales professional has met with a prospect or customer to discuss a project or new offering, but its qualification is incomplete (according to the definition above).

Where all companies get into trouble is at the top of the sales funnel or at the beginning of the sales forecast stages. Why? Sales professionals are under a lot of pressure from multiple sources—the kind of pressure that comes from a career with a substantial proportion of variable income, pressure to be recognized as a winner, pressure from sales management, and so forth. Sales reps love to add "opportunities" to their forecast. The bigger their pipeline, the better they look in everyone's eyes. However, if your organization and people lack forecast discipline, it is a GIGO situation. For instance, you should not add an item to the pipeline of your forecast as "upside" just because you had one meeting and the prospect was interested in hearing more. Statistics won't help you either. You won't necessarily get a percentage of any part of a weakly qualified opportunity.

It's ridiculous to think that you will get good results just from hoping things work out, without doing the real groundwork. Face it, if none of the opportunities in the unqualified upside portion of your forecast ever progress to become fully qualified, then none of them will ever close. After a few meetings and solid initial qualification, these items can become valuable as unqualified upsides. After the work is done to fully qualify them for the quarter, that's the time to include them in the current quarter's forecast. As you can see, this takes discipline, fortitude and patience. It also takes sales leaders who are secure in their game and not desperate to encourage artificially large pipelines.

More discipline is required as opportunities progress through the sales funnel. When an opportunity moves from qualified upside to commit everyone should be able to take it to the bank: The opportunity will close in the current quarter. On the other hand, if an unforeseen circumstance arises and it does not, the sales rep should have another qualified upside opportunity staged to backfill it.

Top–level sales management and CEOs need to be cautious not to force what I call "psychological commits". A psychological commit is given when individuals are backed into a corner and asked to commit their number without being able to list the specific individual opportunities that make up their forecast. I've seen this happen many times, and it isn't pretty. The person exerting the pressure—the "Pressurer"—walks away feeling fulfilled that they've exerted some level of control. The one being pressured—the "Pressuree"—walks away feeling like they are in the middle of the desert without a map and no water in sight They were just asked by their boss's, boss's, boss to commit their quota number, and with varying levels of confidence, they did. Post–cognitive dissonance now dominates their psyche.

Why do we tolerate a lack of proficiency in sales forecasting? Probably because in larger companies, the business is strong enough to hide the issue. However, in small companies, the issue is much more visible. I do think the issue exists in most companies, regardless of size, however, due to the smaller scale in terms of people and opportunities, it is more visible in small organizations. As a profession, I believe we must shift to a more accurate and disciplined approach when it comes to sales forecasting.

Perhaps your company is one of the few lucky ones that doesn't have this issue. If you feel you have accurate forecasting and would like to check the quality of your sales forecast, I will share with you a short process I developed to test the quality of the forecasts of companies my company was considering purchasing. In small companies, you can test the entire forecast. In large companies, you will have to perform a sample audit and test a region at a time.

FORECAST TESTING

1. Obtain a copy of the current sales forecast in a Microsoft Excel worksheet format.
2. Color–code the rows of the current forecast in a specific color. (Say green.)
3. Obtain a copy of the sales forecast from six months ago.
4. Color–code the rows of their old forecast in another color. (Say light blue.)

5. Create a new Excel worksheet and copy all of the rows of both the new and the old forecasts into one consolidated worksheet, keeping the different colors you chose for each forecast.

6. Sort by some commonly–used term or identifier—something they normally use to distinguish each opportunity, i.e. Opportunity I.D., Opportunity Name, etc.

7. Scan the worksheet and look at the stage/progression of each opportunity.

If most of the opportunities have advanced logically forward and up the forecast—from unqualified, to qualified, to commit, to closed—you are looking at a healthy forecast and possibly a healthy business. If the company uses numbered stages, it is even easier to determine what has happened over the six–month period.

On the other hand, if you see opportunities that have not advanced at all, then those opportunities are stalled opportunities. If they have only advanced one level in six months, you can begin to question why. (Although, in some cases, six months is not a long enough period. If that is the case, go back nine months.)

Another area of scrutiny you can test is in the opportunity size or forecast amount data point. Scan the worksheet and look to see if the amount has changed at all over the six or nine month period. If it hasn't, then the opportunity is not maturing at a logical pace. Why? In many companies, almost all original opportunity amounts in a sales forecast are place holders. The reason for this is that it is not until later in the sales cycle that the sales reps have the ability to better define what is being sold, after configuring and quoting the sale. A logical progression would be an opportunity that started out as $200,000 and then six months later was listed as $217,000 or $187,500.

During one of my due diligence efforts on the prospective purchase of a company, I did the Forecast Test, and I recall one specific example to illustrate my point. In the six–month aged forecast, a particular rep in Canada—call her "Jane"—had listed 10 opportunities at Stage 1, each valued at $100,000 Canadian dollars. When I looked at their current forecast,

I saw the same 10 opportunities all still at Stage 1, each still valued at $100,000. My response to their M&A team was that this was not pipeline. On the contrary, it was Jane's "vision". I was thinking silently that it was really Jane's pipe *dream* and not pipe *line*.

In this case, $1 million from one rep in the b.s. column of this small company's forecast was material. It was certainly no joke. When I continued to look at what the rest of the reps had been doing, I found still more issues, and this simple exercise saved my company several million dollars in acquisition cost, since we stalled our purchase long enough to pick the company up for a much lower price than we originally budgeted.

Another forecasting issue is that sales leaders want a pipeline of three times quota. This metric is a key performance indicator of a healthy sales organization. While that is true, I would rather have a smaller pipeline of higher quality forecast items than the opposite. As leaders, we have to be wiser about how we approach these issues and not rely simply on simple answers.

Accurate forecasting is also intertwined with effective sales execution. Remember our discussion of core selling skills? Here is an example of how lack of sales execution can negatively affect a forecast. In one of my former SVP of sales roles, one of the VPs who reported to me added a $70,000 opportunity at a large manufacturing customer for one of our services in unqualified upside. The rep he had hired had failed to ask what the full scope of the opportunity could be, and he and she treated the opportunity as if it were a small scale sale. They did not engage the full resources available or the leaders of our company and align them with the customer's team of evaluators and decision makers. Two weeks before the end of the quarter, the item was moved to seven hundred thousand dollars— that is, it went from a $70,000 opportunity to a $700,000 opportunity!

The VP of sales had all sorts of excuses to my logical questions around how this could have happened. "They expanded the scope of the project," "They expedited their rollout," etc. I knew none of it mattered at that point, since someone else was probably treating it like a seven hundred thousand dollar opportunity, while we were treating like a seventy thousand dollar opportunity.

One of the other SVPs in our company knew the CIO, and the rep tried a Hail Mary pass into the end zone by bringing in the SVP to speak with the CIO. By doing so, we learned that we had lost the sale due to price. You see, our sales rep was only calling on the first level technical manager, while the competitor's rep, who I hired a few months later, was calling on all levels, including the CIO. And she was not working alone, of course, but with her full team of resources and executives. In other words, our competitor was team–selling, treating a large opportunity the way it should be treated, and our rep was not, nor was her manager.

From a forecast perspective, pain, fit, value, and plan were all there, but power was not covered and we were outsold. I had to explain this to my boss, the EVP, and to his boss, the chairman. My EVP described it as a "self–inflicted wound," and he was right. As a champion of accountability, I took the responsibility for the loss and "counseled" the team on how to avoid this situation in the future. However, for the record, it should be noted that if the VP had been doing his job, we would not have lost the sale. He was complicit in letting his rep run stealth, rather than insisting that he visit the account, or have me visit the account at a senior level, as soon as he heard of the opportunity. He should have questioned why we weren't team selling. I guess he should have done a lot of things, but the point here is that forecasts are full of ambiguities, and the best forecasting approach will not produce better results unless the rest of the sales function is working well.

In the case I've just described, the rep was not strong enough in her core job skills, but these kinds of forecasting mistakes can happen even to the best reps. Here's an example from an excellent rep to further illustrate this point. He shall remain nameless since I value his friendship and truly respect his game. He is an absolute "A" player in my book.

Still… here's what happened:

One of my direct reports went on vacation and asked me to cover his forecast call and some of his one–on–one meetings with his direct reports. As I was reviewing the current quarter opportunities with one of the reps, he mentioned what I would label as a "strategic" sale of one of our strategic services to a new account with an impressive logo. I became excited that we were going to close this account.

After hearing the details, I could tell that this person had done a very thorough job on the sales cycle so far. I then suggested that he create a meeting with the CIO of the account to make sure she was comfortable doing business with our company. He said he would. Soon after, I saw that the opportunity was moved to commit status. I assumed he had had a successful meeting with the CIO. Unfortunately, the rep had chosen not to attempt to schedule a meeting with the CIO, since he felt it was unnecessary for a $150,000 order. The clock on the quarter was now running down, and it was time to bring in our business. He was assured by his purchasing contact that he had won the business. They negotiated the Ts and Cs, which takes time and is a great buying signal, so all looked well. But with each day that passed, there was no order from XYZ Company. Finally, the rep pushed hard for an explanation, only to be told that the CIO had overruled purchasing and had given the order to our arch competitor from whom she was buying other services.

Since our rep did not know the CIO, he could not defend his order and his quarry was stolen right out from under him by someone who did very little work in comparison. The rep made a judgment call not to insert an additional step into the sales cycle for so small of an order. However, it was a strategic service and the CIO in this case was engaged. I hate it when I'm right in cases like these.

After all this came down, I spoke to him at length and asked him what he thought and what he could learn from it. I came away feeling that he learned this tough lesson. Of course I was upset that we lost as well, but this was an excellent example of a certain kind of challenge associated with managing sales professionals. In this case, the rep was typically a "scientist" type; however his "artistic" judgment call deviated from the best practice approach we call power–based selling. We'll look into this further in Chapter 18: Hierarchical Selling.

FORECAST VISIBILITY

Before we leave forecasting as part of the Crisis in Enterprise Sales we need to cover forecast visibility. By forecast visibility, I am referring to the view that senior management as well as cross–functional management has into the forecast—not the data in the forecasting system, but the "true" forecast.

Time and time again, I have heard complaints from within companies of all sizes that they lack sufficient visibility into the forecast. They try to follow the quarter's progress by viewing the reports from their corporate sales forecasting system and make projections based on the data they see, only to find after the end of the quarter that the results were quite different from what the data had projected.

The area of most pain with this issue is forecasting across product lines. Ask any VP of product management in a large company, and you will hear this complaint. Most sales forecasting systems only provide an accurate view of the progression of opportunities within a given product area after sales have booked or have been committed. Beyond that, it is anyone's guess, since no one in sales is held accountable on a quarterly basis for achieving each individual product quota. I'm actually not taking a stance on whether they should be held accountable or not. I am, however, suggesting that there is a better way to track the projections and progress on a per–product line forecast basis. The good news is that, if you instill a disciplined approach in your sales organization and get them using dashboards, as I described as our Success Planning process, your product managers and everyone else will have a much clearer view of your business. If a regional sales leader has a dashboard that tracks quarterly progress against his or her goals in total and across all product goals for the quarter, then each region can be consolidated until there is one dashboard. The one dashboard will provide the answers on a weekly basis, which is a great deal better than guessing and waiting until the quarter is over to find out the results.

In our use of the Success Planning sales performance management approach, I am proud to say that any VP of product management or any product manager could pick up the phone and call me to find out where we stood for a particular product on any given day of the quarter. They could also call any of my regional managers to obtain the view for that region. We welcomed those calls and were proud that we had that close a handle on where our business stood. Since we achieved twelve out of our fourteen quarters, most of the conversations were positive. And, in the spirit of "confronting our brutal facts," we communicated our per-product projections openly, whether it was bad news or good news.

Where there was bad news, I would try to roll up my sleeves and dig into the issues with the VP of product management. We would try to understand why that particular product was not selling and come up with a plan to change next quarter's outcome. The sales leaders and staff in my organization knew that they would not be reprimanded for being open and honest about our challenges. In fact, honesty was encouraged. Unfortunately, not all of the sales organizations I have been acquainted with were like that.

I have always believed that organizations should have a holistic relationship between their sales and marketing functions. These two very important functions are interdependent. Yet from an ideas exchange, issue resolution, or forecast sharing perspective, they are often separated by walls. Sometimes the walls are political, sometimes organizational... but walls get in the way of achieving overall success.

Part IV

Opportunity Management

Chapter 17

OPPORTUNITY MANAGEMENT

Opportunity management is the process of managing all stages of a sale from the point of discovery of the opportunity forward, through all the necessary steps until the opportunity is won, closed, booked, and delivered. Common names for the stages in opportunity management are the qualification stage, presentation/demonstration stage, proposal stage, negotiation stage, closing stage, and post sales implementation stage.

Another commonly used term for opportunity management is sales execution, although I would say that sales execution covers opportunity management, plus other aspects of selling. The reason I mention sales execution is because, often when forecasts are missed, leaders often cite the cause as "poor sales execution," when most likely it was specifically poor opportunity management. Before we examine good versus poor opportunity management, let's further define what we mean by opportunity management.

The specific tasks involved in opportunity management vary, depending on what is being sold and whether the customer's buying cycle is structured or unstructured. Here are some of the steps that are likely to be part of the opportunity management in a very structured buying cycle:

- Responding to requests for information (RFIs)
- Attending vendor bidding conferences
- Asking questions
- Qualifying
- Gathering information
- Answering questions about your offering

- Creating proposals and price quotations involved in responding to requests for proposals (RFP)
- Preparing and delivering formal presentations
- Participating in online Internet pricing auctions
- Managing all the aspects of a technical pilot "bake off"
- Negotiating price
- Negotiating legal terms and conditions
- Implementation planning

And so forth...

In informal customer buying cycles, it can be as simple as providing information on your product, negotiating a price, gaining agreement to purchase and scheduling delivery. The more complex the solution, however, the less likely it will be that easy. In general, simple products require fewer steps to manage; complex products require more steps to manage.

A simple example is the sale of new flat screen monitors for personal computers, which requires a discussion of the features of the product as they compare to the specifications the customer desires. It also requires testing in the customer's environment. And mostly it requires competing on price and a delivery schedule.

Compare the personal computer monitor sale to the sale of an enterprise software application, such as various financial applications. Easily over a dozen steps will be required to manage this opportunity. Some of the steps would be interviewing each of the department heads in Finance and Accounting to determine their specific needs from the various modules. Accounts Receivable has a unique set of requirements, as do Accounts Payable, Credit, Payroll, and so forth, throughout the company's financial structure. The sales team has to sell the business benefits of their software, the fit of the applications for each function, as well as the value of their applications/architecture over the competitors. Add to this all the other aspects of a complex sales cycle, and you can begin to understand why sales professionals who are successful selling complex enterprise solutions, such as applications, earn very high commissions. It is money well–earned.

Opportunity Management	Common Mistakes
Qualification	Sales plan not aligned with "true" plan in the hierarchy.
Presentation	Show up and throw up approach because no one interviewed the audience in advance to determine key areas of interest and potential pitfalls to avoid.
Evaluation Pilot (if required)	It's hard to believe but sales teams are often agreeing to pilot without determining the success criteria in advance and gaining a commitment to buy if the success criteria are achieved.
Negotiation	Failure to determine a complete list of concessions the customer is seeking and negotiating off of a complete list. Instead piecemeal
Closing	Not establishing a close plan with the customer and whoever does contracts
Implementation	When a Sales Rep throws a closed opportunity over the "wall" for consultants to implement without involving the consultants early enough in a sales cycle.

Table 1: Opportunity Management Stages and Some Common Mistakes

All opportunities need to be managed—first–time new sales as well as add–on sales or upgrade sales to a repeat customer. However, the latter typically only requires execution of an effective close plan. To try to replicate past successful complex sales cycles, create a best practices approach by adopting a formal sales methodology. A sales methodology is a roadmap defining the steps that were taken, by whom, and when, to manage the opportunity effectively. Let's look at the sample on the next page:

As you can see, just as customers have buying processes, enterprise sales professionals can benefit from having a well–defined, best practices sales methodology. The figure on the following page outlines five phases and the specific actions within each stage. Listed at the bottom of each column are deliverables the sales professional should have accomplished prior to advancing through the cycle. Of course, if a customer leads a sales professional quickly to the closing stage and it is realistic that the customer could buy without going through the previous steps, then the opportunity should be closed. The old cliché, ABC, comes to mind, "always be closing". In most cases this doesn't happen, however, and taking shortcuts only results in a lost or stalled opportunities.

Sample Sales Methodology

phase 1	phase 2	phase 3	phase 4	phase 5
Why Buy Anything?	**Why Buy from US?**	**Why Buy Now?**	**Close Sale**	**Post Sales Implementation**
1. After Lead is qualified by Inside Sales, Sales Rep Phones Suspect and Qualifies the Opportunity.	4. Meet to further identify and establish our value proposition with Business and Technical: Gatekeepers, Evaluators, Influencers, Approvers, Decision Makers, & Signatories.	7. Project Consultant Meets Prospect and Provides Estimate of Implementation Costs.	9. Sales Presents Contracts and Obtains Commitment on Signature Timeframe.	12. Transition to 3rd Party Implementing Or if we are Implementing Go to Step 13.
2. Sales meets Prospect and Completes Qualification Check List. Possible Level 1 Demo.		8. Sales Meets with Prospect Restates Solution Benefits and Gains Agreement on Pricing in a documented Proposal.	10. Legal Approval Process if Required.	13. Sales, Pre & Post Sales Consultants Present Project Plan Document and Obtain Written Sign Off.
3. Sales gains agreement on Joint Action Plan email for evaluating our Solution.	5. Level 2 Demo.		11. Sales Obtains Signed Contract.	14. Post Sales Consultant Leads Project Team Meetings.
Deliverables: Joint Action Plan. Sales Funnel Entry.	6. Pre Sales Consultant Confirms Technical "Buy In" from IT. Deliverable: Functional and Technical Buy In.	Deliverables: Verbal Agreement on Cost of our Solution. Formal Proposal.	Deliverable: Signed Order Form & License Agreement.	15. Sales Maintains Contact with Buyer and Project Head to Ensure Customer Satisfaction. Deliverable: Customer Reference & Project Assessment

Chapter 18

TEAMWORK / HIERARCHICAL SELLING

In enterprise sales, rarely does one individual make a sole decision to purchase a product or service. Typically, several individuals are involved and this project team, whether formally or informally organized, is the hierarchy involved in your opportunity. The hierarchy includes final approvers who are often not divulged to vendors. Many enterprise sales professionals lack sufficient training in how most effectively to assess, analyze, plan and solicit to an organizational hierarchy. I don't view this type of selling to be the most difficult to understand; however, it does require a shift in thinking and acting when compared to a more individual approach.

Rather than just focusing on a primary contact and hoping to obtain approval or, if necessary, meet with that person's manager, situations that call for the team approach require a coordinated team selling effort. However, part of the challenge is that some sales professionals are not comfortable engaging other team members from their company and interjecting these individuals into "their" sales cycle. One thing is perfectly clear, however, the company that does the most effective job of teaming on an opportunity and selling to the power base will defeat the company who does not. (You may recall the two "bad" forecasting stories from the previous chapter.)

The good news is that hierarchical selling is not required on all sales opportunities. Renewal or upgrade sales, if they are not challenged by a competitor, do not require it. Small tactical sales, such as a tool kit do not require it. The easy way to determine which opportunities require hierarchical selling and which do not is to ask yourself, how strategic is the sale? If the answer is, "Very strategic," then it's certain that hierarchical selling is required. I like this filter better than the size of the opportunity, since I have seen many small $50,000 consulting engagements or pilots of technology in very large accounts lead to millions of dollars in revenue downstream. Hence, the first small sales were strategic.

If hierarchical selling determines who wins or loses, and we engage in strategic sales opportunities, then we had better train our people how to do it. I learned it from The Complex Sale, Inc., out of Atlanta, Georgia. Their sales training was the best I ever had. It was the most pragmatic course that had the greatest impact on my ultimate success and income. I've also hired TCS several times to train my people and was very satisfied with their training effectiveness. TCS has a few courses which cover hierarchical selling, and each course lasts two to three days. It is not my intent in this book to try to compete with this type of excellent training. Instead, I intend to explain the general principles of what hierarchical selling is, why it is important, and to share a couple of "war stories" on the subject.

So what does a hierarchy look like? What work does a sales professional do to begin to sell to one? How does a sales professional know they are doing correctly?

Some of the terms I will use are my own terms, and some of them are from The Complex Sale's folks. Their training is so effective that I don't remember which terms are which. In any case you will notice some of the terms are broadly used as well.

A customer buying team typically consists of the following individuals:

The Gate Keeper: This is the person who thinks their job is to hold you and your team at bay. They typically are at a project staff–member level.

The Coach. The person assigned to be your primary point of contact. This person could be from any function in a company, but is often either from the Information Technology Department or the Procurement Department. This is the person who is most accessible to you.

The Evaluator(s). Evaluators are responsible for evaluating the technical fit and/or business fit of your product or service. In the high tech industry, this individual is typically a very technical person from the Information Technology Department. Depending on the culture of the company, they could be very powerful, or not particularly so.

The Recommender: This person is often the project leader, who is responsible for gathering together all of the information created during the evaluation and making a formal recommendation on which vendor to select. The recommender also does company viability research, technical evaluations, pilot evaluations, quotations, and other related tasks and provides a recommendation. If it is to be a decision by committee, then this person will act as the consolidation/communication point. Otherwise, the recommender puts their personal brand behind the decision. The official job title of this person is dependent on the strategic nature of the procurement. In most cases I have seen IT managers or directors assume this role.

The Decision Maker: This is the person who approves the formal recommendation and, in many cases decides, exactly how much is purchased and when. I have never seen a case where the decision maker did not determine generally when a purchase is made. Purchases can get delayed in procurement or legal departments by anywhere from days to weeks, and rarely months, but the decision maker typically calls the shots.

The Approver(s). In all publicly traded corporations, thanks to Paul Sarbanes and the Sarbanes/Oxley legislation, a predefined and documented approval process has been determined and recorded for external purchases from vendors. The size of the purchase typically determines who the approver(s) will be. Small purchases often only require one or two approvals. Very large purchases will require several, and often require the CFO and chairman's approvals. Sometimes approval by the board of directors is required, as well.

The Influencer: A person not in any of the above formal roles who exerts influence on the other individuals on which vendor/product/service is selected. This could be someone within the company who has a strong opinion and enough respect or influence to make it heard, or it could be an outside consultant, hired to advise the decision maker or approver.

The Complex Sales folks refer to the above players as stakeholders, and have created a nifty planning document called a Stake Holder Analysis, which is an excellent way to assess and plan tactics for most effectively influencing a project team. The Stake Holder Analysis prompts the sales professional to question the following:

- ¬ What is the name and title of each of the players in the roles in our buying cycle?
- ¬ What is their "power" in the organization?
- ¬ Do they have a personal/professional agenda? For instance, are they a "lame duck," surfing out retirement? Or a rising star recently promoted looking to make a name?
- ¬ What is their juxtaposition in regard to our product/service /company?
- ¬ Do they need to be supported if they are a supporter?
- ¬ Won over if they are against us?
- ¬ Neutralized if they are against us?
- ¬ Who is the best contact from the selling team to connect with this person?
- ¬ And most importantly, what is the next action item to advance our cause?

If any of these questions can't be answered, which is typical when you are starting a new sales cycle, then TCS teaches us to refer to them as "blind spots". Blind spots are what you can't see, but what you need to find out.

It may be clear to you that this can be pretty involved for a sales professional. However, you want to do anything you can to increase your odds of winning the most strategic opportunities for your firm. The good news, as I've seen it in practice, is that the average high tech vendor probably only needs to do this type of opportunity planning ten to twenty percent of the time.

Another document TCS created is called a "Shark Chart". I love Shark Charts because they help enterprise sales professionals truly see at what levels of their customer's organization they should be exerting influence and spending time, either alone or by bringing their team members into their accounts.

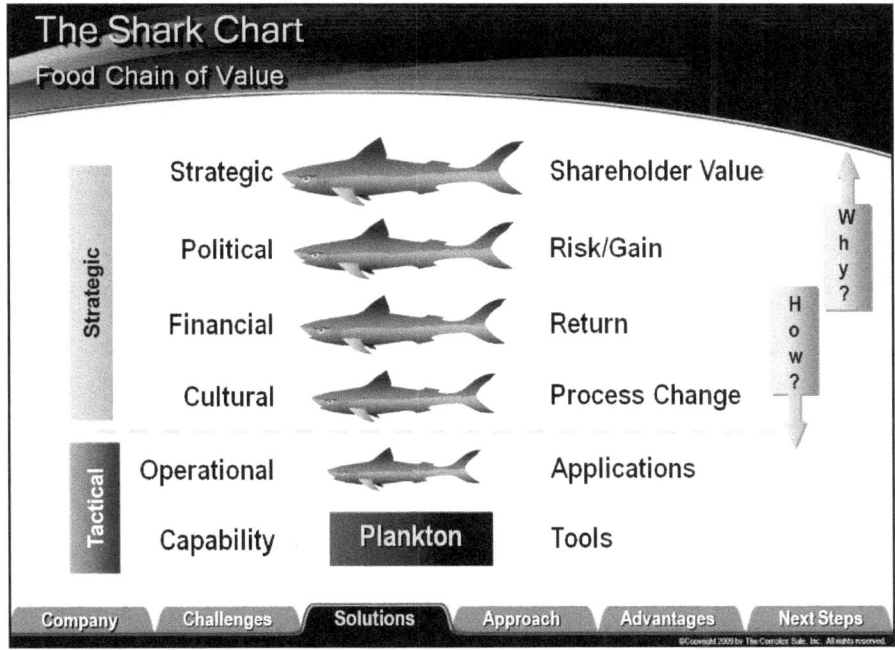

"Figure 18-1: This is what we call the "food chain of values," or our well-known "shark chart" named for the phenomenon that bigger issues tend to eat up smaller ones. Examples of each type follow in this chapter. Executive-level benefits, the ones above the dotted "power line," usually override operational level issues—if the power sponsors are involved. Searching upward for the strategic pain gives reasons for "why" the client needs your operational capabilities. Executives search down for capabilities and tools to answer "how" they will achieve strategic objectives." Rick Page. Hope Is Not a Strategy: The 6 Keys to Winning the Complex Sale. [McGraw-Hill, 2003]. Page 60.

I love to tell the following story of how after years of selling off the cuff, as most enterprise sales professionals are accustomed to doing, I attended The Complex Sales training course and applied hierarchical selling with a more organized approach using their Stake Holder Analysis. In doing so, I closed a million dollars in new business from a new customer.

During The Complex Sales training course, they asked us to use a real world opportunity/account as a way of learning their approach. During my prospecting efforts, I found a billion–dollar–a–year company. Remarkably, no one from our company was calling on them, nor had they heard of this company, perhaps because they were a new entity created after two companies merged, and they had a new name. In any case I was happy to find them. They had a fairly small IT staff, which is always attractive, and after getting my foot in the door I interviewed their director of IT, who was fairly new. I learned that his company was evaluating technologies to implement a data warehouse. My company was not doing any business with this account and competitors were already engaged. We definitely needed to make up ground in this opportunity.

Thanks to my training course, I was invited to take a step back and shape a strategy to apply a team selling approach mapped into the customer's hierarchy. I decided to focus on the chief information officer (Decision Maker), whom I had not yet met, and the director, whom I had met with before. I had my product sales representative and presales consultant focus on the consultant leading the evaluation and the customer's technical staff. This approach enabled me to conduct business–level selling and technical–level selling simultaneously, segmenting our sales efforts. If we had done one and not the other we would have lost.

One of the key reasons we succeeded came from my second meeting with the CIO. One of my call objectives was to invite him to an executive conference my company was hosting with The Patricia Seybold Group. The conference was on data warehousing. I knew our president and COO would be in attendance and mentioned that I would arrange for the CIO to meet and speak with our president. It worked like a charm. He said he was very interested and soon after RSVP'd that he was going to attend.

My competition was focused on selling technology, and I was focused on relationship selling. The CIO came back from the event very enthused about doing business with us. At the event he heard a respected third–party analyst proclaim that we were the way to go, long term, for data warehousing.

I met with the CIO soon after his return from the conference, and we agreed to negotiate a contract. I worked within his budget constraints and sold him over a million dollars in licenses and support, which he purchased in two orders over a period of six months. We became friendly, and he joked with me that my competitor very well may "put a horse's head in your bed," since I did such an end–around on them. They were deeply engaged and working on a pilot, when their sales rep learned that his pilot was being cancelled and they were buying from me.

Of course, it was a team effort, and that's what this story is really about. My team did an excellent job of positioning the strengths of our technology and selling to the techies. And even though they were favoring another vendor, my team established credibility for our technology with them. They also informed the technical evaluators about soon–to–be–released new features that put us ahead of the competition. The CIO also learned this at the conference. When these same techies heard about the decision to go with us, they asked my team, "Who the heck is Dave Govan?" They did not know me, because we took a divide and conquer approach on the hierarchy intentionally, which turned out to be important, since the techies were in bed with the competition.

I influenced the CIO that we were the right choice from a strategy standpoint and our presales team cleared the way for the CIO to lead his team to buy from us. If we had simply skipped the time spent with the technical team they would have been less likely to support the decision to go with us.

The Complex Sales folks taught me how to take what I had been doing and formalize it into a sales strategy and tactical action plan. I soaked it up in class, tested it in the real world, closed over a million dollar sale, and it became religion for me from that point on. Whenever I have hired TCS to train my organizations on how to do the same thing, they have helped everyone who completed their course. As you can tell, I love this type of training. It's not hard to learn, and it can be applied quickly, producing strong results.

Obviously complex selling is not easy, and the above story is an abbreviation of the significant amount of work that we did to gain ground on the competition and win. Navigating the politics and personalities involved on strategic projects in large corporations can be very challenging. Emotions sometimes trump logic or the best technology. Of course, that's all part of the fun. What can be easy, though, is taking a best practices approach like TCS's R.A.D.A.R.®. Most of it is common sense right? Who are the players? What's their power? What's in it for them in regard to the project? Why will they buy from us? Who should we engage from our company/team? Simple questions and often simple answers.

What keeps it really exciting, though, is the human element, which represents the ultimate challenge. Why? Logic often goes out the window. People don't always do what they say or say what they mean. We are constantly having to triangulate with other project team members to validate the information we are being given. It takes a lot of time, a lot of patience, and quite a bit of tact, especially if you have never done business with the particular individuals or company involved in the project. You are basically an outsider trying to become adopted into the community of vendors and suppliers.

The craziest time is near the end of the sales cycle, at a point TCS refers to as "the crucible". I love this metaphor. The crucible is decision and negotiation time. It's the time when a selection and purchase is about to me made. It is the time when the individuals involved are under the most pressure. TCS teaches that, while in the crucible with prospects, one must be prepared to expect any and all reactions, even if they are atypical of the personality of the individuals you have been dealing with for a long time. Anything can happen. Trusted coaches can go silent on you. You may see screaming and arguing. Lawyers can get into fights. It's a time of decision, and therefore, a time of instability.

The way TCS approaches this is to remind the enterprise sales professional that our job while in the crucible is to keep everyone focused on the end goal—to keep things moving forward. We don't engage in any of the crazy emotional interchange. Instead, we allow our prospects to vent, blow off steam, let their thoughts and feelings out. The victorious enterprise sales professional will remain calm at all times, even when the customer has lost her/his cool. As always, I have an example to share.

While in the midst of closing a $20 million enterprise sale that I created, sold and positioned for closure in a current fiscal year, I ran into one unexpected obstacle that ended up creating three dozen obstacles. My Fortune 100 customer decided to engage third–party counsel. As part of the new legal representation, he decided to use my project as a benchmark by establishing a new standard master agreement and three other contract templates. The first problem was that, being a market leader, my company's policy was to work only with our own contracts.

After much internal selling I was able to convince my firm to work off the customer's paper and assign a lawyer to work with the customer's Procurement Department, the third–party law firm and me. I wasn't happy about it all, but neither did I panic. My job was to stay focused on closing large sales within the desired time frame. My compensation plan also governed my behavior, since I would get paid about $250,000 more if I closed the opportunity in month 12 of our fiscal year, versus the following month 1.

So, in a positive spirit, we went into the belly of the beast, and I will attest that it was one of the most difficult and hostile negotiations I ever experienced—and I have experienced countless heated and challenging sales projects. What made it so bad was the third–party lawyer. I would describe him as an "animal" — without doubt, the most obnoxious attorney I ever met. I'm not disparaging his legal abilities. He knew his stuff, but to him, the more one–sided he made the agreement, the better he and his firm looked.

My attorney, who was a nervous chain smoker to begin with, almost had a nervous breakdown. At one point during the negotiations the two lawyers locked horns over some stupid issue and began screaming and cursing at each other. I could be off on some of the expletives, but as I remember it, the invective was flying fast. I remember, "That's B.S.! You are full of @#$*. Everyone knows you can accept this type of term," screamed their lawyer. And from ours: "Go to hell! We are not going to tolerate this type of posturing. I have f*@!ing had it." And my normally friendly attorney got up and walked out.

I apologized to my customer and suggested to him and his lawyer that perhaps we should stop for the day. I also told him I would engage another attorney. So, I calmed my attorney down, tried to provide some words of support for him, and then went over his head to his boss. The next meeting, it was me and the boss attorney—the senior counsel—back in to face "The Animal". This time, we were able to keep the conversation from getting angry or violent, and we were able to work through a number of issues, but we were not making sufficient progress to make our deadline.

Our counsel explained the deadline issue, stating that our progress made it impossible to meet our goals. And my mind was busy with doomsday thoughts, such as, how could I explain to my family that my entire year was a bust? How could I pay for the vacation house I rented? How would I explain a dramatic dip in my income to the market? How could I face my friends who respected my ability to overcome all odds and close big sales?

The answer to all of my internal questions was simple. I could not allow this sale to breakdown over conflict during a legal negotiation. Therefore, I picked up the phone and I called our company president, and he was—thankfully—very supportive. One reason for his support was that I had involved him in the account previously, and he knew and respected their CIO. Also, like me, he wanted to see this deal done within the fiscal year. He knew that an enterprise wide contract with a Fortune 100 company would make an exciting mention on the analysts' call.

The president knew exactly what to do. He assigned his SVP of business operations, who also used to run our legal group, to work personally with me. He also committed to engage personally with the SVP, the customer's team and me to complete the negotiation. Hallelujah! This was exactly what I needed.

I never worked so hard to close a sale in my life. In fact, I literally worked over eighty hours per week during the last two weeks of the negotiation, which was also the end of our fiscal year—this after having worked about sixty hours a week for the prior four weeks. In part, this was because the terms and conditions the customer wanted were so nonstandard that I needed the highest–level consideration and approvals. My whiteboard started with about three dozen issues to negotiate and going into the last day of the fiscal year, which fell on a Saturday, we still had eight left. I was very worried, but somehow was able to get the customers on a conference call with us at 8am, even though it was a Saturday and the CIO was calling in from Spain.

The CIO tried to pull an end–around on me and asked the president for a better deal on price than I had given, but I had warned our president that this could happen, and, besides, we already were offering an excellent price. You should have seen the look on my face when our president gracefully backed me up and said, "Dave has put together a very lucrative contract for you and we should really stick with it." At that point, the phone went on mute and there was silence for what seemed like two hours, but was only a way–too long two minutes. When the CIO came back on he said he was okay where we were and he was prepared to sign off today. My team and I put our phone on mute, only to erupt into shouts of joy and exultation! We high–fived each other. We hugged each other. We screamed at the top of our lungs! Nine months of very hard work and tremendous stress had just produced an awesome outcome for everyone involved.

Oh, but wait a minute. We're not done yet.

Our signatory, EVP of legal was pissed off at us for kicking his attorney's off the project, and he refused to sign it. Come on! What the heck do I do now?

Back to the president. "Dave, I am in a hotel in Dallas getting ready to go to my daughter's wedding. You have thirty minutes to fax it to my room, and you better make it 'drunken sailor simple' on where I am supposed to sign.

I sheepishly replied, "Actually I also need you to initial every page of the fifty page contract." The tension in his voice conveyed to me that I had better bust my butt to get this to him now or sooner, and I did. And, at last, we were done.

My team and I each earned whopper–sized commissions. I was nominated and awarded Global Account Manager of the Year by our executive committee. I received the award at an awards dinner in a massive ballroom in a castle in the city of Barcelona, in front of several thousand other employees. I was given a unique custom–created glass sculpture, and I received a double promotion to regional manager. It doesn't get much better than that.

The customers, by the way, got an excellent contract that enabled them to leverage our technology across their organization for five years, without the expense and hassle of sporadic license acquisitions. My customer friend in procurement and the IT project head were both promoted to director. And "The Animal" got his agreement established as the software and services buying agreement for a Fortune 100 company—not to mention his hefty fee, as well. To quote a former manager, "I had a full head of hair when this sales cycle started…" .

Throughout the hellish negotiation process, I thought about my young sons and the song, "Mothers, Don't Let Your Sons Grow Up to be Cowboys," kept going through my head—only it was enterprise sales professionals I was unconsciously substituting for "cowboy," even if the meter didn't scan so well. Now, I have four sons, and I hope none of them ever has to deal with such craziness.

While we just looked at an example of how emotions can complicate hierarchical selling, what about when emotions remain mostly calm, but customers do not do what they say they are going to do on the close plan? One of my absolute favorite stories is about a former colleague and business friend and what he had to do at the last minute to close a mega enterprise sale in a Fortune 100 account. Like the previous example, he had been working on the sale for months and had done an excellent job positioning everything to close on time. His legal negotiations, while very challenging, fortunately did not break down, and he was able to complete the negotiation without all the issues I ran into. However, the last part of the close plan did not go as expected.

My friend's VP–level contact had informed him that all final signatures would be completed within the desired timeframe. He was patient and professional and followed up every day. Each day his contact updated him that another signature was obtained. (By the way this type of issue happens all the time) Finally on the last day of our fiscal year, conveniently located at the beginning of a long holiday weekend, only one last signature was required. According to the customer's policies an officer of the company had to sign off on it, and the CFO was prepared to provide it. This was long before Sarbanes Oxley, which in recent years every public company has established as the formal approval processes. There were only three officer–level candidates in town that week, but "Not to worry," his contact said. "The CFO has it on his agenda to sign it today."

Finally just after lunch, my friend's patience had worn thin and he pressed his contact for an update. "I have bad news for you," his contact began. "The CFO has left the office unexpectedly for the long weekend, and he cannot be reached. This will just have to wait until Monday." He added, "I'm sorry. I really tried, and I did everything I could do." His contact continued, Not to worry though. There is no chance of us not signing this contract. We need the licenses. We have the budget, and all approvals are done except one signature."

My friend, a strong New Yorker type, was about to lose a few hundred thousand dollars in commissions and face the same risks I cited earlier. His hunter passion took over and he told his contact that he was jumping in a cab and coming down to his office. Together, they were going to walk the halls until they found an officer to sign off on the agreement. He was not taking no for an answer.

Meanwhile, my friend's new manager, who I like and respect, but who came from a different company culture, insisted on accompanying him and jumped in the taxi with him. I'm sure he wanted to make sure that there was not a negative impact on the relationship, but he did not have the same financial incentive as my friend did.

So off they go from midtown to Wall Street in a New York taxi. The whole time they are in the taxi, my friend is trying to visualize a successful outcome, while his new boss is trying to sell him on backing off. Finally my friend has had enough and he yells, "Pull this cab the f#@$ over!". The

driver pulled over. My friend opened up the cab door and said, "Sam, get
<expletive> out of this taxi. I am going down there. I am going to find
someone to sign this contract, and I am getting this deal done today!
Goodbye". The new manager, in total shock, jumped out and off went the
taxi without him.

Next, the company contact tried to talk him out of it, but my friend
sold the guy on escorting him up to executive row. He also threatened firm-
ly that tomorrow the same order would cost millions of dollars more. Up
they went, and down the hall the walked. The contact spotted an officer,
and my friend—very calm and friendly—asked for two minutes of the officer's time. He explained how hard and long the project teams from both
companies had worked to bring the contract to closure and how one minor
issue was threatening their success. He asked if he would please sign for
the other officer.

The guy asked his colleague, who was standing there, if everything
else was in order, and with an affirmative reply, he signed the contract. My
friend came back to our office with the order in hand, told us this unbe-
lievable story, and we all burst into applause and shouting. What an awesome display of tenacity and passion. What an awesome display of performance under pressure!

Are you shaking your head in disapproval after reading the story I just
told, thinking it represents short–term behavior that risks long–term relationships? Think again. Public companies rely on accurate forecasts to be
in the investment community's favor. CEOs rely on their sales organizations
to meet their forecasts. My friend would never have committed this item
unless he had several assurances from power players in his account that this
would get done in time. It was an eight figure contract. It was a committed
item. It had to get done. Okay, so no one's life would be ruined if it didn't.
Worst case, some reps could get fired, and people have been fired in such
cases, but that is rare. In this case, my friend was not at risk to be fired, but
a massive portion of his W2 was at risk, and that, my friends, made all the
difference in the world. Everything we or our families had was from what
we earned, and as you can tell we worked darn hard for it.

Okay. Enough stories for the moment. Let's look at how to resolve this crisis point. It's really straightforward. Organizations should distinguish between tactical sales and strategic opportunities. On the latter, organizations should deploy trained and experienced enterprise sales professionals. Those sales professionals should create a hierarchical sales strategy for the opportunity with a very specific tactical sales plan that engages and leverages a team of individuals at all levels in their company. If your product or solution is strong enough to compete, but not necessarily the best available, and you execute an effective hierarchical sales strategy, you will defeat your competition nine times out of ten—unless, of course, your competitor is executing a more effective hierarchical sales strategy.

Chapter 19

ACCOUNT / TERRITORY PLANNING

Despite the fact that things can go wrong, even when you have completed all the necessary preparations, in many cases, things go wrong simply because of poor planning. I've already talked about planning to manage and win opportunities, but there is one other type of planning that seems to be going by the wayside in many companies, thus further contributing to our crisis—namely, account planning. By definition, account planning is the creation of a plan that communicates the following:

- Account Name
- Account Description / Background
- Account Team Members
- Historical Sales from the Account
- Current Year Sales Targets for the Account
- List of Identified Projects or Areas of Opportunity
- Detailed Description of Top 3–5 Major Opportunities
- Hierarchical Sales Strategy/Action Plan to Win Each of the Major Opportunities
- List of Resources Required to Compete and Win Each Opportunity
- Description of Alliance Partners Engaged With Us On the Account

As you can imagine, given this list of deliverables, it is only feasible to do account planning on the largest accounts. Also, if a company has only one solution to sell, account planning may be overkill. This is why you typically see account planning done by large technology vendors who have a lot to sell and who have a good sized team of sales professionals focused on large accounts.

Here is a sample account plan I like to use. It includes most of the items above. However, since this report did not have historical revenue or account–specific revenue targets, those sections are not listed.

XYZ Account Plan

For:

By:

Date:

I. The Account

A. What are the major industry trends and key busi- ness indicators within the accounts industry?

B. What is the growth strategy of the corporation?

    Acquisition:

    Additional Market Share:

    Stop Decline:

C. Who are the Customer's primary competitor(s)?

D. Who is the corporate audit firm and managing partner?

II. Your Customer's Customers:

A. Who are your primary Customer's Customers?

B. Define your primary Customer's Customer.

C. What value proposition impact and competitive advantage can you have on your Customer's Customer (i.e. Full Product Suite, etc.)?

D. Define your strategy for supporting your Customer in order for them to better support their Customers.

E. Provide C "x" O, VP and key contact background info.

Title	Name	Phone	Relationship (years)	Last Meeting
CEO	--	--	--	--
CFO	--	--	--	--
CIO	--	--	--	--
VP Legal	--	--	--	--
COO	--	--	--	--
VP Purchasing	--	--	--	--
VP HR	--	--	--	--
VP Manufacturing	--	--	--	--
VP Research	--	--	--	--
VP Marketing	--	--	--	--

F. What are the three top corporate initiatives/objectives and what impact do they have on the organization?

1.

2.

3.

III.   Finance

A. Provide key Finance Management Information:

Title	Name	Manager	Phone
CFO			
Controller			
AR Supervisor			
AP Supervisor			
IS Liaison			

B. What are the top initiatives/objectives of the CFO?

C. What financial applications are they running and for how long?

D. What reporting tools do they use today?

E. What countries do they operate in? How many currencies do they utilize?

F. Do divisions operate independently and how/when do they roll up to the corporate books?

G. How do they interface with IS?

IV. Information Systems

A. Provide key IS management information:

Title	Name	Manager (years)	Prev Employer (years)
CIO			
DBA Manager			
VP (Application Development)			
Architecture Planning Committee			
End User Liaison			

B. What are the top initiatives of the CIO?

Business

Technical

C. Which IS function is designated to interface with end users? What is their role?

D. Who funds the enterprise and end user applications?

E. Who is responsible for evaluating and acquiring horizontal technology (i.e. end user, IS, committee)?

1) Monitoring:

2) Reporting:

3) Collecting:

F.List IS strategic partners in the following areas:

	Vendor	Rep
Legacy Systems		
DB		
Development Tools		
Ad Hoc Reporting		
DSS		

G.List 5 key influencers in IS and who they influence:

Influencer   Title

Influence   Title

etc.

V. Purchasing

A.Describe the purchasing cycle once a decision to buy technology is made. (i.e. end user purchasing legal final signature cycle)

B.What signature level does the CIO, CFO, CEO have?

CIO $

CFO $

CEO $

Others:

$

$

TOP THREE OPPORTUNITIES

It is also important to discuss the top three opportunities in your account plan. You should include a chart similar to the one on the following page for each of your opportunities, listing the details of each opportunity, customer contacts and resources you require to win the oppoprtunities.

TERRITORY PLANNING

Account planning is not always called for, but in those cases where account planning is not warranted, an enterprise sales professional should have created and be working off of a territory plan. A territory plan is very similar to an account plan; however, instead of planning to penetrate one or more large accounts, the rep is planning on penetrating a geographic territory. Territory planning is the creation of an annual plan which communicates the following:

- Territory Description (Geographic or Vertical Boundaries)
- Segmented list of Large, Medium, and Small Accounts in the Territory
- Sales Team Members
- Historical Sales from the Territory
- Current Year Sales Targets for the Territory
- List of Identified Projects or Areas of Opportunity
- Detailed Description of Top 3–5 Major Opportunit es
- Sales Strategy/Action Plan to Win Each of the Major Opportunities
- List of Resources Required to Compete and Win Each Opportunity
- Description of Alliance Partners engaged in the Territory.

Again, as you can see from the above examples basic planning can assure focus and optimal productivity from your sales organization. So you might wonder why we have we gotten away from account or territory planning. I think of it this way: In most companies, we are all engaged in managing our manager. That is, we are accustomed to giving only what our

Hierarchical Selling Strategy: Opportunity One

Opportunity Name	Customer Name(s)	Opportunity Value	Products Offered	Competition	Issues/ Challenges	Success Criteria	Resource Requirements
—	—	—	—	—	—	—	—
—	—	—	—	—	—	—	—
—	—	—	—	—	—	—	—
—	—	—	—	—	—	—	—
—	—	—	—	—	—	—	—
—	—	—	—	—	—	—	—
—	—	—	—	—	—	—	—

managers require and not much more. In sales, we are quite independent. We tend to resist "paperwork". If a company or manager does not require account or territory planning, we may or may not do it. After all, it's "paper-work," and it's optional. However, the better performers plan anyway, since they know planning equals success and success equals commissions.

I remember being in a job interview once and being told by the hiring manager that his boss was concerned that I might be too laid back for the job. I asked him to get me in front of his boss ASAP. They were having a Saturday offsite, and I was given thirty minutes during a break. I spent a few hours creating a sample territory sales plan the day before and went over it on Saturday with the VP. He asked me if I created it on my own. I said I did and that it was something I always do. In this case, I was not an insider and it was just a sample, but it was enough to communicate to the VP that I knew what I was doing—not to confuse polite and professional with being too laid back.

But isn't this really just common sense? Fail to plan, plan to fail? Once again, the most common excuse given for not creating a plan is that it takes time away from selling. Obviously, it's just not true. I take this as such a rhetorical point that I am embarrassed that I even have to discuss it here. However, if I don't flag the issue, it may be overlooked.

I think part of what happened over the several decades that companies have been doing account is that many account plans evolved to become inflated documents, produced once for sales leaders to review, after which they became "shelfware". In other words, they sat on the shelf in the account manager's cube and were used only when asked for by a manager. Sales professionals on very large accounts produced one–hundred page account plans with tons of data in them. Account reviews grew to half–day meetings. I believe this still occurs with a few large vendors, by the way. The point is, account plans became encyclopedias instead of plans of attack. No wonder people didn't want to do them.

So, here's another simple resolution for this crisis point: Leaders should require planning. And if you don't think your reps are capable of planning, get new reps who are. If your sales organization is too small or too young for account planning, you can still do territory planning. If you are large, then you should be doing account planning. If you are growing, you should be preparing to add account planning to your overall plan.

However, when it comes to the bloated plans that have become all–too common, I believe that less is more. Companies need to develop a format for account or territory plans that limits the size and focuses on just the pertinent ten points I've already described. Inform your sales organization that plans, and the reviews of those plans, are required. If you are the CEO of a small or medium–size company, I suggested informing the sales organization that you would like a copy of each plan. If you are in a very large company, you can delegate this down to a feasible level.

Any time you or your staff is asked to go out to visit an account or territory, you should be able to have your assistant provide you with a copy of the plan from the files. Further, plans should be reviewed twice a year, once at the beginning and once in the middle of the year. Size and scale will determine who does the review and how often. Again, this is an example of performance management at work. Plan, coach, assess... This isn't rocket science, and I really shouldn't have to be harping on it like this. Sales organizations should just do it, but too many of them don't.

Part V

Human Capital

Chapter 20

STAFFING

Staffing is another major crisis point in the enterprise sales profession. Anyone who has ever staffed sales professionals for their company, or has worked as a contingency–based recruiter—even someone who has retained a search firm for a sales leader—knows exactly what I am talking about. I saved staffing for last because I wanted to be sure you understood all of the other areas of the profession that are in crisis. So it makes sense that if there is a crisis in how we perform in the enterprise sales profession, it's largely because we don't have people who are doing things the right way. So, where do we find these people? Now you see the problem. Seeing how so many areas of the profession are in crisis, you can imagine how difficult it is to find and recruit high–caliber enterprise sales professionals and leaders.

It should come as no surprise, then, that staffing is a significant issue. If you doubt it, try talking with any sales leader or any recruiter and you will hear the same response: "It is very hard to find great people." Let's examine that statement. Why is it hard? Why aren't most candidates great?

I suspect that the problem stems from inadequate training, as I mentioned earlier, and from ineffective communication between hiring managers and recruiters. Hiring managers are not spending enough time creating accurate job descriptions and explaining the job specifications. In some cases, they may not fully understand the requirements, themselves. In other cases, they have not been trained to be more specific. But isn't sales just selling? We already know that, at an enterprise level, the answer is no. Is baseball just baseball? No. Not all baseball players are experienced at playing every position. They don't have to be, but what about enterprise sales professionals? Am I saying that there's more than one position in enterprise sales? Yep. Here is a quick rundown.

Title	Description
Territory Manager	Manage a geographic territory. Prospect in hundreds of accounts.
Account Representative	Manage a named set of accounts.
Global Account Manager	Manage one large account.
Product Sales Specialist	Support other sales reps by selling a particular set of products.
Sales Consultant Presales	Support of other sales reps.

There are other titles and responsibilities, of course, but this list captures several important ones.. So the question is, does the sales leader have the right jobs spec'd out for his/her business, and, if so, are they asking for those candidates whose experience and skills best fit the job? I think by now you fully understand that experience and skills vary in all professions, and this is clearly the case within enterprise sales.

Back to the baseball analogy In the Major Leagues, outfielders could probably play first base in a pinch, but first basemen typically don't have the experience to play center field. Each position varies. I just think about A–Rod and his struggles switching to third base in his first year with the NY Yankees. Well, you can see that I enjoy my baseball analogies, but it's true that each position has its own challenges and skill requirements—in baseball and in enterprise sales.

So, what are we talking about here? What are the characteristics and expectations of each position on the enterprise sales team?

Territory Manager. "Hunter" personality, travel oriented, high sales call volumes, sales spread across many accounts. Knows how to open doors. Heavy prospecting.

Account Representative. "Farmer" personality, knows how to develop deeper relationships, great at cross–selling, strong at long–term support.

Global Account Manager. Same as Account Rep with Management and large deal abilities.

Product Sales Specialist. More technical aptitude.

Sales Consultant. "Techie" with a personality, strong demo skills.

If we can agree that there are differences among the roles and jobs on the enterprise sales team, ranging from subtle differences to DNA–level traits, then we can probably also agree that sales leaders should be looking for the right people, with the right traits, for the right jobs. Moreover, when you're working with a recruiter, you can see that it's a good idea to spend some time explaining the assignment and which skills and experiences are needed, not in general terms, but for that specific job assignment.

Of course, this is just the tip of the iceberg. If you want to be as successful as possible, take into account more variants, such as the issue of provinciality. For instance, New Yorkers selling in the Midwest are not as effective as Midwesterners selling in the Midwest.

Over the years, traditional large companies like Xerox, IBM, and others have scaled back their college recruiting and new hire sales training programs. Young college graduates, or young professionals out in the workforce, definitely suffer from the lack of opportunity to go through extensive training as part of their employment. I'm not citing myself as the prototype of sales excellence, but one edge I share with many of my friends who are now in their forties was the opportunity to receive extensive training early on. This kind of training simply is not the norm today. Just for context, I'm going to give you a brief description of my education and training background, which occurred over a period of years and in different companies (on next page):

1. Received two weeks of formal sales training at first job. Received two years of sink or swim OJT in direct sales with a downtown New York/Wall Street territory.

2. Assigned a formal mentor in the field. Spent six months of formal sales training, three months away at a training center, and three months in the Field OJT. While away I was videotaped and reviewed during simulated sales cycles almost every day. I received formal classroom training on every core sales skill mentioned earlier in this book. After being deployed to the field, I was required to take a minimum of ten business days of training every year. Advanced courses on negotiation, selling to CIOs, how companies are led, product training, etc. While calling on pharmaceutical accounts, I was trained as part of a class by the FDA for a day on how drugs are brought to market and approved. I was recognized as a candidate for executive education and sent to Babson College for an intense two–week executive education course on Managing Complex Opportunities. The instructors were all PhDs from Harvard, BC, Babson, and BU.

3. Required to take five business days of training every year. Trained on hierarchical selling, more presentation skills training, more negotiation skills training, training on how to sell to global accounts for international experience and more product training. As a regional manager, I recieved training on how to manage within the law but, surprisingly, not leadership training.

4. It was the Dot Com boom. A bit of product training. Most training went out the window. Trained on managing within the law again, just in case enough fear of being sued without company support was not instilled in me the first time. (I never had a single HR issue, but companies were told to provide this training to limit their liability in the face of sexual harassment suits.) I provided sales training to my sales org or presales and sales.

5. No formal training but heavy OJT on how to raise money and how all functions of a software company are managed. I provided hands–on training to my team of sales, presales, and consulting.

6. As part of chairman's extended staff received excellent formal leadership training at chairman's off sites and at three formal leadership training events from Noel Tichy, author of The Cycle of Leadership. Included a 360 degree evaluation and project work.

As you can see I have been fortunate to receive quite a bit of training throughout my career. Some companies offered little training, but others more than made up for it. Let's face it, none of us are born with the knowledge and experience needed to sell, manage, or lead. Some of us have certain attributes or an upbringing that enables us to excel at certain aspects of the enterprise sales profession, but I strongly believe that there is no substitute for training.

I believe we have a staff quality crisis because we have not invested sufficiently in our human capital by providing training, nor have we recognized the need for formal mentoring. Further, we have a staffing crisis because hiring managers are not communicating with enough specifics about the requirements for each particular open enterprise sales job. In turn, many recruiters do not possess a deep enough understanding of enterprise sales. Often, they also lack knowledge of the specific segment of the industry their client is in, so they aren't able to ask for more specific requirements and then filter candidates accordingly.

The point is, in the case of enterprise sales there are specific and unique job assignments, and each requires unique traits, skills and prior experience. When recruiting, it's really important to measure candidates against those specific requirements. Unfortunately, far too, many people are totally missing this point. They are hiring to general requirements, not the specific requirements that will make all the difference once the person is put on the job. Not only do we have a quality and experience issue in the candidate pool, but we are consistently putting people in the wrong jobs.

Here's a typical example: A company decides to expand a particular sales organization, so they budget accordingly and tell the sales leader to write the job descriptions and post the jobs. The sales leader writes up a general one–size–fits–all job description and works with an internal staffing person or a third party recruiter to locate candidates, conduct interviews, evaluate candidates and hire someone. It all sounds pretty straightforward, so where is the breakdown? Let's look at the dialog that might occur between the sales leader and the recruiter, and maybe you'll spot the problem.

> **Recruiter**: "Thanks for giving me the opportunity to recruit for you. Let's now spend some time and go over the job profile for your ideal candidate's experience and attributes."

> **Sales Leader**: "I need a Hunter".

> **Recruiter**: "A Hunter? Is that what you said?"

> **Sales Leader**: "Yes. Exactly!"

> **Recruiter**: "Do you have any other specific requirements?"

> **Sales Leader**: "I also need someone with a strong track record."

> **Recruiter**: "Anything else?"

> **Sales Leader**: "Yes, the person must live in or near Dallas and be willing to travel to Houston."

> **Recruiter**: "Okay. Got it! Thanks. I'm on it!"

You may laugh, but this is not an oversimplification. It is far too common. Many contingency recruiters I have known love overly general job specifications. Why? Because it is much easier to just keep throwing general candidates at a hiring manager until they pick one—much easier than having to work through the filters to find the right person for the right job. I have had many of these individuals tell me that I am so hard to recruit for. Why? Because I really know what I want. Give me a break.

So, back to the recruiting process. What was missing? Perhaps some specifics would help:

- Is the new hire selling in a geographic territory or to a named set of accounts?

- Or would they be managing one large account?

- Maybe they will be only one of several reps on a large account team?

- Which vertical industries must the person cover?

- How complex is the product they are selling? Would they need prior experience with that kind of product?

- What type of training do you want them to have had in the past?

- Do you need high velocity sales with smaller average sales prices or large complex sales over a longer period of time?

- Is the person an overlay product rep or a line sales rep?

- Does the job require hierarchical selling?

- How much money do you want them to have earned in the past?

- What type of personality are you looking for?

- How many years of business experience?

- Do you want a senior rep or a junior rep?

- How much are you prepared to pay them?

- Do they need to come from one of your competitors or from any other specific segments of the industry?

- Do you want to hire future leaders?

- Are they going to sell all of your products or just some?

- What values or personality in a candidate would constitute a good cultural fit?

- Is there certain upbringing you are looking for?

- Is there a certain look you are looking for?

- Are there specific companies you would want them to have worked at?

- What level and type of customers will they be calling on? Techies, Executives? C level? All of the above?

- What level of internal employees will they be interacting with on the job? Middle Management, Senior Level Executives?

- What size sales do you want them to have closed in the past?

- Can you afford and are you looking for a top 10% rep or a 100% to 120% consistent performer?

- What type of references does the candidate need to produce; for instance, do you require customer references as well as job references? Which levels?

- How many jobs is it okay that the candidate has had in the past?

- How many years experience in your industry?

- Do you want experience in specific accounts or a specific territory? If so how many years?

Perhaps you don't have to ask all these questions, but you can see that the short dialog I provided was wholly inadequate if any reasonable number of these questions needed to be answered. And, to be honest, this was little more than a stream of consciousness core dump, yet I added three dozen additional filters which, if answered, would improve your chances of finding the right person for the right job. Compare that with the original three filters. Some sales leaders may go beyond three filters and go to 10, but unless those 10 are more specific than general, the issue of overgeneralization is still going to exist.

I'm sorry to say that I have seen far too many strong sales leaders blow this part of their game. As a result, they take too long to staff up, and their staff's performance is lacking because they hired the wrong person for the job. Honestly, it's not easy. Sales leaders have plenty of other work to complete to perform their job function, and effective staffing can be a full–time job in itself. Internal and external recruiters are not off–loading on the sales leader, though. They simply lack sufficient knowledge of the sales profession to do much of the sales leader's staffing work. Further, for all the reasons I've already covered in this book, it seems that the number of great candidates gets smaller each year.

It's hard to find the highest caliber reps. They are the ones who aren't out there looking for a job. They are too busy earning strong commission. The ones who are great, but are in transition inside a company, are often "tree hugging" – trying to get a better gig in their current company where they know what to expect, rather than move into a new and unknown situation.

Once again we ask ourselves, what we can do to resolve the crisis?

Can management science help here? One answer to this problem is to help our hiring managers and recruiters be more specific by using a simple technique I developed. I call it a Candidate Evaluation Matrix. Here is an example I created for the mythical XYZ Company (see next page).

As you can see on the Candidate Evaluation Matrix, we have asked the hiring manager to list the specific job requirements that we are going to use to measure our candidates. We will provide this same list, but not the form, to the recruiters.

As you can see from the matrix, I have listed common hiring criteria for an enterprise sales executive. I have also weighted each criterion with a 1 for low, 2 for medium, and 3 for high degree of importance relative to the specific assignment I am recruiting for at that time. For instance, if I am recruiting for a territory manager covering a broad geography, then ability and willingness to travel is weighted a 3, for high importance. If I were recruiting for a named account representative based in a major metropolitan area, then the same criteria would be weighted with a factor of 1 or low importance because travel is probably only occasional.

Next, you will notice that candidates are scored on a scale of 1–10, with 10 being the highest score. I have found it very useful for the same candidate evaluation forms and scoring methods to be used by all parties who interview the candidates. This prevents the process from becoming a beauty contest of subjective feedback versus objective feedback based on the job specifications.

Getting back to the travel example, let's say Candidate A is interviewing for two open sales jobs, territory manager and account representative, which is not uncommon. Candidate A expresses a dislike of business travel and scores a 2 on a scale of 1–10. In the Territory Manager Evaluation Matrix, the weighting factor for Travel is 3, and the highest score possible

Candidate Staffing Evaluation Matrix

Candidate's desired skills, experience, and attributes	Level of Importance for this Position (3 = High, 2 = Med, 1 = Low)	Candidate's Score (1 = Lowest, 10 = Highest)	Total Score (1 = Lowest, 10 = Highest)
Fitting in at XYZ, Inc.			
1 Perceived fit with XYZ Inc.'s culture and values	3	10	30
2 Start up sales experience	2	5	10
3 # of years enterprise software sales experience	2	10	20
4 Scored high on profile test	3	10	30
Experience: Related to XYZ, Inc.'s Needs			
5 Sold technology as a business solution in business departments AND I.T.	3	10	30
6 Number of years relevant information technology industry sales experience	3	5	15
7 Experience within your specific industry segment	2	5	10
8 Past productive account relationships within to be assigned territory	3	5	15
Experience: Job Performance			
9 Consistent track record of achieving bookings greater than $2 million year.	3	10	30
10 Track record of closing ____ deals per quarter of ____ dollar size.	3	5	15
11 Outcome of verified customer reference check.	2	10	20
12 Outcome of back channel reference check.	3	10	30
Sales Skills & Formal Training			
13 Perceived ability to prospect and obtain ____ meetings per month	3	10	30
14 Understands & utilizes Power Based selling approach on strategic opportunities	3	10	30
15 Ability to engage in detailed, complex, multi-year contract negotiations	1	10	10
16 Presentation skills	3	10	30
17 Uses a thorough qualification process when qualifying opportunities	3	10	30
Personal Attributes			
18 Communication skills: listening skills & verbal skills	3	10	30
19 Likeability and strong personal & professional presence / charisma	3	10	30
20 Passion for excellence in customer satisfaction	2	10	20

Candidate's Total Score   465

Minimum acceptable score 85% of total possible score   451

Total Possible Score   530

for this criterion is 30 (10 x 3 = 30). Since Candidate A only scored 2 x 3 = 6 out of a possible 30—there is clearly not a good fit for that assignment. However, for the account manager role, the highest score is 10 or 10 x 1. Candidate A's score of 2 x 1 is 2, only 8 points off of the highest score for the account manager job, but 24 points away from the best score for the travel criterion for the territory manager role. Since the travel criterion is far more relevant to the territory manager's job, it is significant that he scored so low, and might be enough to disqualify the candidate for that job. Since travel is not so relevant to the account manager's job, its relevance would be overshadowed by other criteria, such as the complexity and size of opportunities closed or the caliber of the accounts he or she managed. Each would be more significant in determining the candidate's fit for account manager. However, the key thing to keep in mind is to look at the aggregate score when comparing candidates.

This is a simple illustration, but you can see, taking this approach across a dozen or two criteria, how the weightings for a specific assignment will provide a better assessment for optimal job match. I don't expect sales leaders to become statisticians, but if they just apply a bit of management science to help filter candidates better, they are more likely to put the right people in the right assignments.

This isn't purely theoretical, either. I've seen mismatches first hand, and they are painful for everyone involved. Frankly, mismatched job assignments are a waste of precious human capital. Here's a quick story of a classic mismatch that illustrates my point:

A young and talented employee does extremely well in inside sales, selling one product. Jim knows everything there is to know about that product and the market and is promoted to outside sales in the field, initially in the right job as a product sales specialist (also known as an "overlay" sales rep supporting other sales reps in the field). Jim thrives in this new position and earns over $300,000.

The next year they eliminate Jim's job and assign him to be the account manager in Manhattan for several of the largest financial services customers in the world. This was shortly before I joined the company. After I began working there, I was informed that Jim was struggling, so I spent time with him, quickly grew to like him, and observed him first–hand in the field. After a short time, it became clear to me that he was in the wrong job. He didn't know enough about the other products to sell them. He wasn't strong at opening doors, nor was he strong at closing new business.

Jim's skills didn't match his job description. That's all it was, and it wasn't his fault. No one leaves the womb with intrinsic knowledge, but instead learns through training and experience. It was painful interacting with him during one–on–one sessions because he wanted to improve, but did not know how to do so. Our mutual way out of the issue was that I lobbied my manager to allow me to make him an overlay across my Eastern sales organization for the next fiscal year. After I positioned it, not as a setback, but as a vital role on the team, Jim went with the reassignment and added tremendous value across the entire organization. I could have easily forced him out of the organization, but we would have lost a great person—someone who worked hard, is smart, was loved by customers and colleagues alike, offered great ideas—and all those qualities, talents and experience about our product and industry would have been lost. Instead we all benefited from putting him in the right assignment. The right person for the right job. It changes everything.

Another serious issue within staffing of enterprise sales talent is not performing background checks. I'm not sure why many firms don't perform background checks, perhaps they are trying to avoid "offending" a candidate. However, I would not trust my customers and/or business to individuals without having had their background validated. We all know that a lot of people lie on their resumes. And many candidates leave off unsuccessful sales jobs. Sometimes people stretch the truth a little to make themselves seem better. When you read a person's resume, you can factor in a little self–promotion, but sometimes the falsehoods go far beyond stretching.

Fairly recently I almost fell for a pathological liar's game. He looked great, he sounded great, and his references were great. Fortunately, one of my recruiters warned me about the lies, and I called one of his previous managers—someone I knew personally—who verified that he was lying. I won't go into the details, but it would have been a disaster to have trusted this man. The point is, they are out there—liars, and tricksters and BS artists just waiting to BS you.

Here's an example of a time when I did make a bad hire. I did not use a Weighted Scoring Matrix, I had too few consensus interviews, and I went against my gut instinct. It happened at a time when we were desperate (first problem) to hire someone in an important vertical where we had some business, but not enough. There was tremendous upside in this vertical.

I knew someone who worked for one of our alliance partners, and this person approached me for a job. The need for a hunter was of high importance for this assignment. I knew the firm she came from was not known to have many hunters, so three times I pushed back in different interviews and conversations. I told her that I didn't see her hunting skills or abilities, and that I was not comfortable. However, she was relentless. "I'm a hunter, I'm a hunter, I'm a hunter" is all I kept hearing. She offered a mutual customer reference, who I respected tremendously and who seemed to believe she was a quality enterprise sales rep. We had no other candidates to go with at the time, so I approved her hire to work for one of the VPs in my organization.

What a mistake! She had the lowest sales call volume I can recall in a long time. She could not open doors. She did not build a pipeline. She was not a hunter. We had a leadership change in that group and the new leader figured her out quickly, monitored her closely, put her on a performance plan, and ultimately removed her from the organization. Bottom line is she lied. I gave her every opportunity to withdraw gracefully from the interviews, but she refused. She said she was someone she was not—someone who was accomplished at opening doors and obtaining new sales appointments... someone with strong prospecting skills able to build a pipeline. She was not any of those things.

Occasionally, everyone makes a bad hire. It's the nature of the beast. However, if you use consensus interviews and a weighted scoring matrix, you can increase your odds of success.

SALES DEPLOYMENT

Once you have the right people, they need to be optimally deployed. Most established corporations tell sales leaders where they want their sales resources deployed. Younger companies rely on the expertise of the sales leader for deployment. I don't view this as an area in crisis; however, I want to mention a few pointers to growing companies.

1. Follow the money. Don't deploy in verticals that are not currently spending unless your product helps them with their current issues. E.g. Automotive in 2007.

2. Double down in those verticals that are spending money. For instance, prior to the market crash, I would be referring to financial services. Goldman Sachs Research for the Tech Sector found that the top three verticals spend about two–thirds of their entire budget on technology. Those verticals used to be Financial Services, Communications, and Manufacturing.

    In the current state of our wounded economy, it appears that government, healthcare, nondiscretionary consumer goods, and entertainment seem strongest. However, I haven't seen any research that validates their level of proportionate spend on technology. For example some areas of entertainment, such as online gaming, spend heavily on technology, while traditional media companies are not big spenders when it comes to technology. They would rather spend money on producing content.

3. Filter for the highest propensity to buy your particular product or service. In other words, reality versus what someone else tells you should be happening.

4. Deploy your precious sales resources in market "sweet spots". Using direct sales for market research is a costly proposition. Time is money.

5. Don't overlook certain geographical areas just because they may not be well known in your company. I joined a division of a Fortune 1000 company that had no sales heads deployed in TOLA

(Texas, Oklahoma, Louisiana, Arkansas or Ohio Valley or Pittsburgh or St. Louis).

6. Alliance Partners are a cost effective way to get more feet on the street.

7. Put the right people in the right jobs!

COMPENSATION

While this is a very broad topic, it is important to mention it is a crisis point. The following research conducted by Deloitte Consulting in 2005 and contained in their brief, "Maximizing the Effectiveness of Salesforce Pay," found that a majority of sales leaders are dissatisfied with the returns on their sales compensation programs. In the brief, they said,

> "Due to dissatisfaction with their sales compensation programs, organizations made a number of changes to their pay plans in 2005, with the objective of increasing the effectiveness of these plans. Given that redesigning the sales pay plan and effectively communicating these changes to employees are costly in both time and dollars, this is a concerning trend. Furthermore, these modified pay plans are not guaranteed to succeed, inviting the possibility of additional changes with even greater costs".

I have yet to see any positive reversal concerning this trend in any of the past few years since 2005. Perhaps the enterprise sales profession has yet to mature to the point of stability when it comes to compensation but the thing to keep in mind is when sales compensation programs are changed each and every year not only is it very costly but it steals time and focus away from selling.

Part VI

Crisis Resolution

Chapter 21

CRISIS RESOLUTION: WHAT TO DO NEXT

Why should we let such important functions in a company continue to operate without taking a best practices approach? Clearly, there are solutions and winning strategies. The first, and most straightforward thing to do is to look for opportunities to apply management science within your sales organization, or, if you are an individual contributor, within your own sales game. Hopefully, you are convinced of the effectiveness of this approach from what you've read here. It makes so much sense.

What's the worst that can happen if you try these methods? Attrition? If you are delighted by the sales productivity results you are getting across your sales organization now, then I'm guessing that you are doing many of the things I've suggested here. However, if you are not delighted, then it would see that you have a lot to gain and little to lose.

The rest of this section will provide you with some assessment tools and processes that I am sure will increase your company's sales efficiency and productivity. Let's start with finding out what problems or issues are present in your company. Where are you at? Are you satisfied, or looking for improvement?

Let's start by reviewing your current state and assess areas of improvement. To begin with, I'm going to ask you to list the business issues you are experiencing, the perceived root cause and the corrective action.

Here is an example of the template I use:

ASSESSMENT METHOD

BUSINESS ISSUE:

Forecast accuracy from a timing perspective. Too many opportunities slip from one quarter to the next.

Root Cause(s):

- Lack of consistent forecast classification. Reps are using different terms to describe the status of opportunities.

- Lack of forecast discipline at rep level and manager Level in regard to qualification of opportunities within a particular quarter.

- All upside is treated as fully qualified for current quarter which is not possible.

Corrective Action(s):

- Establish consistent opportunity classification: Booked, Closed, Commit, Qualified Upside, and Unqualified Upside

- Direct sales leaders to segment opportunities into the above five categories and manage their sales teams closely to ensure this forecast discipline is adhered to and that forecast items are scrutinized closely for power and plan.

ENTERPRISE SALES IMPROVEMENT CHECK LIST

If you are responsible for sales directly or indirectly in a company, then you should review and assess your organization against the checklist on the following page.

Enterprise Sales Improvement Check List	In Place?
The right Sales Reps in the right jobs	
Effective Sales Leaders	
A Professional organization living Company Values	
Bi-Weekly Performance Coaching of Reps by Managers	
Coaching off of a tracked Key Performance Indicators Dashboard	
Pipeline Size relative to Quota	
Established Cross Product Targets and Cross–Selling Progress	
Sales Call Volume	
Disciplined Qualification: Power and Plan most importantly	
Weekly Forecast Update Calls	
Forecast Discipline i.e. Qualification, Timing, etc	
Hierarchical / Team Selling approach on strategic opportunities	
Account Planning / Territory Planning	
Opportunity Management / Close Planning	
Sufficient Quarterly Recognition	
Effective communication of job specifications on staffing	
Use of candidate evaluation matrices when interviewing	

SELLING DURING A RECESSION

When I started writing this book, the economy was softening. As I complete the project, there's no question that we are in a full blown recession. Therefore, I would like to share the following advice on how to succeed in sales during a recession.

I've sold through several down markets during the past twenty–four years. I managed to make my numbers every year except two or three times when I changed jobs. Since I never changed jobs during a recession, I was able to achieve or exceed my quota in all down markets I faced. If your income is dependent on sales success in our current economic climate here's a Top Ten List of suggestions to help you weather the recession.

1. If possible, align your sales assignment to adapt to changes within industry verticals.

    If you are a named account manager in financial services, you should be sharing the account intelligence you are gathering about your customer's policies on expense and capital spending for the rest of 2008 and 2009 with your highest ranking sales leader. The financial services vertical is in disarray. Management has a responsibility to adjust to the economic conditions. In some cases this may mean redeployment to other verticals in other cases reductions in quotas, changes in compensation plan structures, etc.

2. If you are not locked into a particular vertical, focus on verticals that are not wounded.

    According to Gartner Group, IT spending in enterprise is predicted to increase by 2% in 2009. Companies rarely stop spending entirely in down markets. Pursue verticals and companies whose businesses overall are healthy, but are merely cutting back to deal with the recession—for instance, defense, healthcare, government, certain consumer packaged goods, life sciences, online gaming, media & entertainment, etc.

3. When selling to accounts with businesses that are healthy or at the very least, still functional, find the projects that are labeled as critical to the business.

These projects are unlikely to be cut. Pursue only those projects and pursue them vigor.

4. Make sure you are selling something that is truly needed and of high value.

Now is not the time to be selling solutions searching for problems.

5. Increase your sales efforts.

Work harder to fully understand what issues your Prospects are dealing with during the recession and think of ways your product or service could help them.

6. Use Value Based Selling.

During recessions, all project spending receives closer scrutiny. If you are selling something that is on the pricey side of life, your customer has to build a financial business case to justify their spend. To seal the deal, your proposal should include a Return On Investment Analysis that you create with your customer. This can be a good closing tactic as well. Present a draft ROI and ask for his or her input on it. Make sure your ROI focuses on hard ROI and not soft ROI.

Many businesses like to use complex ROIs, and that's fine, but if your proposal can pass the simple ROI test, you're on the right track. An example of a hard ROI is: Buying Solution A will result in an incremental gain of X and expense reduction of Y. An example of a soft ROI is: Buying Solution A will increase customer satisfaction, boost competitive advantage, etc. An example of a simple ROI is: Simple ROI = (Gains less total cost of ownership) divided by the total cost of ownership.

So what do you do?

1. Be cool and don't panic.

Stressed out and anxious sales professionals spread anxiety. When a prospect voices concerns about the economy, acknowledge the concern and show empathy. Then respond with a positive data point that you can attribute to a credible source;. i.e. transition to a positive topic/ice breaker before discussing your opportunity. You need to influence your prospect's outlook in a positive way and redirect them to your solution after they have shifted to a positive frame of mind.

2. Be flexible.

If your prospect wants to start small, then start small. If flexible payment terms are needed, then provide them. Now is not the time to be rigid. It's the time to close the sale at all costs as soon as you can.

3. Fight like crazy to win the business.

Don't be eliminated by competitive price discounting. Work with your prospect closely to find a creative solution for responding to competitive attacks through price discounts. Be willing to discount, but try to counterbalance it with longer–term contracts with pre–negotiated price increases or minimum volume commitments. You can also try to hold your price, but give away additional products or services at a 100% discount to counter the competition, thus maintaining your opportunity value.

4. You can never have enough partners.

If your sales call volume decreases due to customer access challenges, instead of spending that time commiserating with your sales colleagues in the office, spend your time with your alliance partners or other vendors who are engaged in your accounts and may have insight or leads for you. Also, spend time with colleagues of your target prospects to gain additional account intelligence to help you find recession–proof projects.

Summary

In Summary

It's time to get real about the issues surrounding enterprise sales. Recognizing the crisis and increasing the visibility of the problems we face will elevate the discussion to a higher level of importance and help reveal the negative impact it is having on the performance of many companies. Examining the root causes of the crisis challenges us to look deeper into our sales organizations and how they function. And finally, understanding the most effective solutions to improve or resolve the issues enables us to initiate the necessary actions and apply resources needed to resolve the crisis and to maintain a healthier company.

Taking action to resolve the crisis requires courage and tact, particularly if you have never been part of a sales organization. During the past two decades I've seen leaders and staff from non–sales functions view enterprise sales and its inner workings in a variety of ways, ranging from contempt to mystique. Given the current issues inside the sales profession and the negative impact these issues can have on other peer functions, such friction is understandable. At the same time, when one recognizes some of the exciting achievements sales has accomplished, it is not surprising that sales is sometimes held in awe.

Some sales leaders and professionals I've known appear to enjoy the mystique surrounding how they do their jobs. Unfortunately, mystique includes mystery, and mysteries and businesses don't belong together. When you unveil the current state and the inner workings of enterprise sales, with the exception of a small percentage of overachievers, you find a profession dependent on undertrained and semi–disciplined sales professionals practicing their art without consistency.

There are a number of root causes, which were examined throughout this book:

- **Culture**

    Many companies lack an effective sales culture to provide an optimal environment for sales. While many sales professionals exhibit solid values and strong professionalism, many others need work in both areas. As I showed in Part I of this book, organizations that have an effective sales culture, based on strong core values and professionalism, will have an excellent foundation for over achieving.

- **Core Selling Skills**

    Unfortunately, in all but the largest companies, sales training during the past two decades has been cut back dramatically. Less training has lowered the level of proficiency of core selling skills among sales professionals. Effectiveness at core sales skills such as Prospecting, Qualification, Presentation Skills, Negotiation, and Closing have noticeably decreased over the years. Likewise, management effectiveness is a major part of the problem.

    The solution, as I showed in Part II of this book, is more and better sales training. Whole generations of sales professionals have lacked sufficient training, but investment in training will pay off in more ways than one.

- **Performance Management**

    Along with other core selling skills, the interaction between many sales leaders and staff has yet to evolve to a point where both parties feel comfortable openly discussing key performance indicators and metrics and strategizing in a more functional player/coach dynamic. Instead, any attempt to implement such elements of management science often gets labeled as micro management, and both parties retreat to the limitations of typical sales forecast meetings. Performance management aspects of management science are rarely applied in managing sales organizations, but they can and should be.

Dramatic results can be obtained by applying a little management science. I have proven over the past eight years that performance management dashboards for enterprise sales are not only effective, but they have played a major role in producing excellent results and in some cases turning struggling company sales organizations around. The process I created is called Success Planning, which I introduced in Chapter 13. Success Planning is a dashboard–based approach that empowers individual sales contributors to more closely monitor progress against goals and other key performance indicators set by sales leaders. Additionally, these dashboards are the backbone of weekly coaching between the sales professional and mid–level sales managers. Improved visibility and coaching helps improve Sales Productivity, Pipeline Volume, Deal Sizes, Cross–Selling, and Sales Forecast Accuracy. These ideas are beginning to achieve broader acceptance; for instance, well–respected management consulting firms like McKinsey are now recognizing the benefits of this type of approach.

- **Sales Planning**

  Another root cause of the crisis is the lack of planning around sales calls, managing opportunities, team selling, working an account list or working a territory. Certainly not all, but many, sales professionals are consistently in reactive mode. Poorly planned sales activities tend to fail. Shifting to the practice of proactive and thorough planning will increase sales win rates. Throughout Parts III and IV of this book, I dealt with the issues and solutions surrounding sales planning for success and opportunity management.

- **Human Capital**

  Sales Professionals and Leaders are among the most precious assets your company has, yet time and time again I've seen major issues in staffing, deployment, and compensation, all of which are detailed in Part V of this book. More scrutiny and depth is needed when creating job specifications, interviewing, and hiring for your sales staffing needs. Once hired you need to make sure you are putting the right people in the right jobs when deployed. Sales compensation is another area that requires greater attention and I believe expertise. Make sure an expert helps you get it right. It should not be left to the subjective opinion of one individual.

- - -

The good news is that resolution of the crisis is within our control if we invest in two primary areas:

First, we must train our sales professionals to make up for any deficiencies and to empower them to succeed using all the tools available to a well–trained sales professional.

Second, we must apply management science principals of performance management, coaching and planning. These principles must be applied in a disciplined way, simultaneously blending harmoniously with our sales culture.

The checklist introduced in Chapter 21 will guide you to focus on the right areas to resolve the crisis as it exists in your company. I am confident that if a company effectively implements these solutions, methods and strategies, they will resolve the crisis for themselves. If the industry itself adopts these ideas, we can resolve this crisis for once and for all, and that's why I wrote this book—to help the enterprise sales profession evolve and achieve its fullest potential.

INDEX